DO NOT REMOVE
CARDS FROM POCKET

VGM Opportunities Series

OPPORTUNITIES IN
WRITING CAREERS

Elizabeth Foote-Smith

Foreword by
William Brohaugh
Editor
Writer's Digest

 **VGM Career Horizons**
a division of *NTC Publishing Group*
Lincolnwood, Illinois USA

Cover Photo Credits:
Front cover: upper left, Scotland Yard Books,
Ltd., photo; upper right, *Dayton Daily News*
photo by Sol Smith; lower left, © *Writer's
Digest*; lower right, University of Iowa photo.

Back cover: upper left, photo by Jane Scherr;
upper right, Northwestern University, Medill
School of Journalism photo; lower left, ©
Writer's Digest; lower right, Columbia
University photo.

Foote-Smith, Elizabeth.
  Opportunities in writing careers.

  (VGM opportunities series)
  Bibliography: p.
  Summary: Basic information for the would-be writer,
discussing jobs and salaries according to the current
literary situation and according to projections for the
future.
    1. Authorship—Vocational guidance. [1. Authorship—
Vocational guidance.   2. Vocational guidance]
I. Title.   II. Series.
PN153.F66   1988   808'.02'023   88-60909
ISBN 0-8442-6512-8
ISBN 0-8442-6513-6 (pbk.)

Published by VGM Career Horizons, a division of NTC Publishing Group.
© 1989 by NTC Publishing Group, 4255 West Touhy Avenue,
Lincolnwood (Chicago), Illinois 60646-1975 U.S.A.
Library of Congress Catalog Card Number: 88-60909
Manufactured in the United States of America.

8 9 0 BC 9 8 7 6 5 4 3 2 1

ABOUT THE AUTHOR

Elizabeth Foote-Smith wrote her first piece of fiction at the age of ten. But though she continued over the years to write poetry, short stories, and plays "just for the pleasure and the challenge," years passed before she considered a professional writer's career.

Instead, in response to a strong impulse toward music (and with a minor in music from the University of Minnesota), she became first a composer performing her own music, then a piano instructor, and finally a professional jazz pianist.

After receiving a bachelor's degree from Northwestern University and a master's degree from the University of Chicago in English Language and Literature, she spent five years teaching—English in suburban Illinois high schools, and literature and writing courses at the University of Wisconsin—where, finally, she determined to become a full-time writer.

Her publications include poetry, short stories, and three novels, two of them mysteries published by Putnam. *Opportunities in Writing Careers* is her first published nonfiction book.

ACKNOWLEDGMENTS

The author gratefully acknowledges the assistance of the following in the preparation of this book:

Barry Hanson, Corporate Communications Department, Associated Press (AP); James Briggs, Director, Career Counseling and Placement Center, University of California, Berkeley; American Advertising Federation (AAF); International Association of Business Communicators; The Newspaper Fund; Louise L. Wesley, Main Library, University of California, Berkeley; and Marlene Nesary, Dorothy Bryant, Norman Jayo, Barbara Wood Donner, Lawrence Fortenberry, Sally Kao, Carol Pearson, Dan Sidhu, Timothy J. Smith, M.D., Miles White, Norman Wilner, and Cynthia Yaguda.

FOREWORD

I envy you. You're standing in the stacks of your library, maybe sitting at a table, or at your desk. You've found *Opportunities in Writing Careers* on the shelves, or a teacher or friend has pointed it out to you, and you're feeling the excitement. It's an excitement of possibilities, of creative challenges, of putting your love of words to use. A novelist— maybe that's what you want to be. Or a poet. You see bylines in your favorite magazine and wish they were *your* name. You have true or made-up stories in your head, and you want to sit at a keyboard and tell them. I envy you because I've stood where you stand now, different book in hand, but the same dream within me.

I've also been where I hope you'll follow: receiving my first acceptance letter, seeing my first play performed, receiving the magazine with my first byline in it. I hope you discover as I did the wide range of writing you can do. I have word processor disks filled with novels, and I've written my share of serious plays. But I've also written children's theater plays, articles on how to play video games, comedy skits for local disc jockeys, puzzles and word games, a menu for a local restaurant.

Some of that was for money. Some of that was just for fun.

And you can expect fun in this business. You *cannot,* however, expect glamour. Writing is hard, demanding work. You must master grammar, vocabulary, the basics of storytelling, the delicate yet powerful implications of a single word. This is the profession of the artist, yes, but it's also the profession of the craftsman. If you are to follow me into this profession, you will encounter the same obstacles I did.

And you will discover many of the same rewards. You will perhaps sell that novel, touch people with that poem, move them with that play. You will perhaps inform the public with your news coverage or with your science or technical writing. You will perhaps write ads or press releases, movies or TV shows, greeting cards or the backs of cereal boxes—which, if you're like me, is where you started doing much of your regular reading.

But what you won't do is write the foreword to *Opportunities in Writing Careers.* I've already had the honor of beating you to that one.

William Brohaugh
Editor
Writer's Digest

PREFACE

You are considering the writer's profession. You have a talent. You have developed some writing skill. And, most important, you *enjoy* writing. But choosing a career or changing careers is a serious step. In order to make an informed and intelligent decision, you feel that you would profit from some guidance in the form of an overview of the opportunities such a career offers. Then, too, you would like a realistic appraisal of the obstacles and hardships to be confronted.

Whether you choose to be a free-lance writer or a salaried writer, this book is designed to provide basic information that you will need to make your decision. It describes the current literary situation and offers projections for the future. It approaches job descriptions, job opportunities, earnings, and salaries from a realistic point of view. It includes profiles of interesting people at various stages in their careers. It asks of you that you read carefully, assessing yourself and estimating your personal potential as you read. It is hoped that this book will answer your important questions, help you to clarify your thinking, and offer you an enlightening picture of the writer's life.

DEDICATION
To Carol, Timothy, Christy,
Adrienne, Larissa, Heather,
and Hana

CONTENTS

Writers must be tuned to the temper and tempo of the times, the cultural and economic peaks and troughs. (Dayton Daily News photo by Sol Smith)

CHAPTER 1

INTRODUCTION

A word is dead
When it is said,
Some say.
I say it just
Begins to live
That day.
— Emily Dickinson, 1872

Writing is a form of communication. To create a written composition is to create a message. If a writer's message is to reach the minds and hearts it was meant for (as Emily Dickinson's has), it must be published and publicized in the literary market place. It must be printed, read, heard, viewed, and discussed.

The writer's market is never static. In some areas demand far exceeds supply; in others applicants far outnumber available positions. If you aspire to join the work force of writers in this country, either in a salaried position or as a free-lance writer, you must be tuned to the temper and the tempo of the times, the cultural and economic peaks and troughs.

In recent years there has been an atmosphere of flux and unrest in the publishing business. Integrity, many writers believe, has been too often sacrificed in the interest of profit. There is a deep concern about the welfare, even

1

about the survival, of a tradition of thoughtful, meritorious literature.

In October 1981, an American Writers' Congress was assembled to discuss the crisis. The issues to be confronted were concentration in the communications industry which threatened to exclude and silence serious writers; new writers' difficulties in finding publishers; government's slashing of funds for the arts; libel suits, book bannings, and censorship by special interest groups.

Crises in the arts are nothing new. Life, as Hippocrates said, is short; art is long. Individuals may succumb, but writers are not an endangered species.

Nothing can take the place of the written word. And if it is true, as we are told in Proverbs 25:11, that "a word fitly spoken is like apples of gold in pictures of silver," think of the implications for words fitly written!

How did writing evolve from the crude pictures and symbols of the far past to the diverse literary forms of our age? For when we think of writers and writing, we commonly think in terms of literary genres—short stories and novels, plays and poetry, articles and reviews, all the various forms which touch our lives as we encounter them in the newspapers, magazines, and books we read. How did this amazing phenomenon called writing begin?

When humans formed communities, language resulted. Because the spoken word could not be preserved on tape or records as it can now, writing evolved. This evolution, of course, consumed an enormous span of time.

Many ancient peoples were so awed by the magic of writing that they attributed its invention to their gods. But for writing, the spoken languages of the past would have vanished. We have reconstructed them from scratchings on flint and figurines, pottery, and pebbles, wooden tablets and building blocks. Without writing, imagine how few of the cultural achievements of our ancestors would have been preserved and handed down through history.

Today we can preserve the spoken as well as the written word. We can project our voices and our writings to unknown beings on satellites in galaxies we may never penetrate. Some space traveler in a future age, encountering our time capsule, may ponder our symbols and scrawlings and listen with astonishment to the strange sounds of our language.

Today we have the telephone, the phonograph, the tape recorder, motion pictures, and television. Yet we cannot now, and may never be able to, dispense with the written word, even if we wanted to. The preservation of our past depends on the billions upon billions of words on tablets, pages, records, film, and microfilm stored in the archives of libraries and other cultural institutions around the world. The record of the present must also be put down in linear fashion, word after word, whether by pencil, pen, typewriter, or video screen, to preserve it for the future as well.

Today's writers research, analyze, and recreate the past. Their objective reports and imaginative insights deepen our comprehension of the present, its major and minor events, its ideas, beliefs, and opinions, its achievements in art, science, technology, and social progress, its conquests and catastrophes.

Nothing can take the place of the written word. In our complex culture, skilled, intelligent writers are needed perhaps more than ever before.

Top: Getting a college education is important for those who are serious about being writers. (University of Iowa photo)

Bottom: Students learn about book publishing in a discussion with the president of a publishing company. (Radcliffe Publishing Course photo)

CHAPTER 2

WHY WRITERS WRITE

Below, mostly culled from interviews of well-known authors, are some answers to the question, "Why do writers write?"

> "There seems no reason for my having become one except an irresistible inclination . . ."
>
> Somerset Maugham

> "I want to change the world . . . it's why I write."
>
> Alvin Toffler

> "Oh, I think I became a writer because I love stories."
>
> Eudora Welty

> "I write basically because it's so much fun . . ."
>
> James Thurber

> "It's as if God put me on earth to write . . ."
>
> John Gardner

It could be that one overriding, and perhaps unconscious, reason writers write is to learn—surely to learn about the external world, but also, and perhaps primarily, to learn about themselves. For the process of discovering who you are is the process of becoming a more distinct, knowledgeable, and secure being.

Writers write to communicate, to instruct, to entertain. Some write for the gratification of acclaim. For them, Robert

Louis Stevenson offered a word of warning, calling popularity an "empty and ugly thing," though he considered praise from other artists "one of the essential and enduring pleasures."

In a February 1980 interview in the *Parisian Review,* author Norman Mailer advised, ". . . obviously it's important not to take a book on just because it promises money. You can go down the tube very quickly by that route."

But the professional writer does write for money, though it is hoped not just for money, or the writer may come to resemble Arnold Bennett as Virginia Woolf described him. He had, she said, "a shopkeeper's view of literature." And he was "covered over with fat and prosperity."

Though money pleases, the professional writer who refuses to "sell shoddy for broadcloth," as Anthony Trollope wrote, will ultimately be esteemed.

Given a list of suggested motivators or motivations for becoming writers, respondents of a survey, all of them members of P.E.N. (a world association of playwrights, essayists, editors, and novelists), chose as follows:

the need to write	282
literature: reading a particular body of work	212
a teacher	99
fame	76
wanting to be a part of the literary community	72
not wanting to work 9–5	55
a strong role model	49
accidental	24
financial opportunities	17

Perhaps, after all, William Saroyan was right. ". . . No writer knows," he said, ". . . why he writes; he only likes to imagine that he knows."

THE GENESIS OF A WRITER

". . . the arrangement of words—the music of rational speech which is in man inborn, which appeals not to the ear only but to the mind itself . . ."

Longinus

"There are in America 200,000 persons cherishing aspirations toward the settin' down job of authorship."

Upton Sinclair, 1927

Have you ever pondered the question of when, where, and how you got the urge to be a writer? For you do want to be one, or you wouldn't be reading this book. Are a certain percentage of people born with a genetic predisposition to write? Is the writer's career the product of environmental influences? Is it heredity, environment, a devious collaboration of both, or some other mysterious factor? Let's look at the so-called "facts."

Heredity

Longinus seems to have credited heredity. Could heredity have provided the impetus in the case of Anthony Trollope? Although Trollope, born in 1815, grew up, as the *Encyclopaedia Britannica* put it, "in an atmosphere of decayed gentility, mingled with recurrent financial worry," he might very well have planned his writing career *in utero,* for his mother, in addition to Anthony and his two brothers, had more than fifty novels in her.

Charles Lamb's father was a scrivener. Mary Shelley's

father was the formidable writer and thinker, William Godwin. (We will overlook, for the moment, the environmental influence of Mary's relationship with Percy Shelley.) The father of Denis Diderot, chief editor of the brilliant French *Encyclopedie,* was a master cutler, which may or may not account for Denis's incisive style. Mere anecdotal evidence, you say? Then let us turn quickly from nature to nurture.

Environment

Parents can often, inadvertently or not, provide an environment conducive to the shaping of writers. Bronson Alcott, Louisa May Alcott's father, may have been perennially poor, but he chose to live across the road from Ralph Waldo Emerson, whom Louisa May visited from time to time. And Henry Thoreau's father was a manufacturer of pencils.

Many of the world's finest writers grew up in a threadbare milieu, parented by indigent fathers and ignorant mothers, and subsequently developed the melancholy or choleric temperaments of Coleridges and Kafkas. The forebears of others were depressingly wealthy.

Mutation

There you have the case for nature and nurture. Not to be overlooked is the slim chance that a writer might be a sort of one-shot literary mutant. For example, consider the case of a writer born into a family, all of whom as long as any of them can remember, had grown up to be bricklayers. A tidy analogy could (but won't) be drawn between wordlaying and bricklaying.

Although the one-shot mutation hypothesis seems the most credible choice, the question of a writer's genesis remains a baffling one.

THE SYMPTOMS

There are certain suggestive symptoms to be observed when a writer's career is in the making. Children who grow up to be writers often show susceptibility to infatuation with words and word patterns at a very early age. I once knew a small child (now a writer) who was so taken with spelling that she used to memorize new words feverishly each day as she skipped happily to school. On one occasion I asked a class of young persons to write a *haiku,* an unrhymed Japanese poem with an intricate problem of word patterning. The children returned the next day, grubby, wrinkled paper in their hands, pride in their eyes. Two or three (those destined to be poets) could be more nearly described as being in shock.

Addictive reading is another major symptom. Incipient writers usually begin perusing the world's literature at a very early age. Think of John Stuart Mill, who during his first two years, must have read everything in the English language that was appropriate to his age, for by the time he was three his father was teaching him Greek, and in his seventh year he began reading Latin.

A third symptom appears when an innocent, healthy-minded person becomes victim to infection by a book. Certain books are infectious to susceptible persons. Could you have been one of these? Perhaps your reading was fragmentary, until one day, when you were six, or maybe sixty, you read a very admirable but subversive book. It might have been *Alice in Wonderland* or Conrad's *Heart of Darkness.* Whatever it was in your case, you had never been so engrossed. When you put the book down, your mind was reeling with questions: "How did the author go about it? Why did he begin where he began? How did he contrive to make his vision my vision?" Then came the crucial question: "Is it possible that I could learn to write so well?"

Then what? Were you satisfied just to wonder? If so, the attack was acute. It passed. But if from that point on you found yourself obsessing over the structure and stature of each book read, pondering the author's style, probing the syntax, gauging the quality of the ideas, and (even more critical) slavishly aping these facets in scribblings of your own, either you have been scheming to become a writer, or you are one.

There's another symptom—chronic scribbling. Stevenson, obviously a chronic scribbler, lived with words. He practiced constantly. To be a writer, one must read, he believed, for writing alone "set no standard of achievement."

Persistent, intense reading and writing are two prerequisites, then, to becoming a professional writer. "I kept always two books in my pocket," Robert Louis Stevenson wrote, "one to read, one to write in. As I walked, my mind was busy fitting what I saw with appropriate words . . ."

THE BENEFITS OF A HIGHER EDUCATION

If you are serious about becoming a writer and you don't have a college education, it would be wise to get one. It is true that neither Shakespeare nor Ben Jonson were university graduates. Mark Twain didn't have a college degree. Georges Simenon and William Faulkner never finished high school. But we live in a world buried beneath the debris of a media explosion. It has been snowing paper ever since Gutenberg's printing press, beginning with the tiny, intermittent flurries of the fifteenth century, thick with Bibles and prayerbooks, right on through the mass-produced snowstorms of the nineteenth century to our interminable twentieth-century blizzard. During all that time (and long before, for that matter) some superior writings have been composed by some superior minds. So as writers, we need to read, understand, and appreciate the standards of our predecessors, the better to reflect upon and establish our own. Only shallow writing springs from superficial minds.

> "As in the body, so in writing, hollow and artificial swellings are bad . . ."
>
> Montaigne

Some quite intelligent and profitable reading is done in English literature classes at colleges and universities, where students collectively discuss and analyze individual books and writers and learn about their historical and social backgrounds. It is a revelation to study the anatomy of a great novel. It isn't at all like the study of medical anatomy. The purpose of an autopsy, for example, is to find out what went wrong. Conversely, as a result of a skillful literary "dissection," life is created. Studying the book as an organism, we examine its structure, its various systems and parts. We probe to its very heart. And thereby we discover its soul. (For every great book has a soul.) And then, excitingly, it comes to life. For this kind of dissection animates and enlivens almost forever such unforgettable characters as Tess, Huck Finn, Emma Bovary, Molly Bloom, Oliver Twist, Lady Chatterly, Raskolnikov, and myriads of fictional characters, some of whom we know and understand better than our closest friends.

The same thing holds true for nonfiction. A desultory reading can be as meaningless as a glance at a passing stranger.

A college education, then, though not indispensable, could be important to a writer's future. If you cannot finance one, there are loans and scholarships to be had. And if you must work during the day, there are evening schools where you can earn a bachelor's degree at your own pace. If possible, choose an institution with a strong creative writing, journalism, or communications department.

If you are already enrolled in a university or college and are considering a major in writing, but want to explore the opportunities further, visit your school's career information center. At the Career Planning and Placement Center, University of California at Berkeley, I talked with Director Jim Briggs to learn how such a center might help in defining career objectives and planning goals.

"Step one," he explained, "will show the student how to determine whether his interest is a valid one."

Step two involves using the resources of the career center library for some in-depth reading. Step three puts the student into direct contact with people working in his or her field of interest.

As the student investigates aspects of journalism, he or she will be reflecting on his or her own fitness for such a career. When the student's career interest is properly focused, Mr. Briggs told me, "he will want to discuss how to reach his goal." That will entail selection of his or her major and the coupling of academic work with practical experience.

If you are planning to study writing at the university level, get copies of the annual bulletins containing courses of study at the college or university of your choice. Look in the index under English, Creative Writing, Communications, or Journalism, depending on your interests. For example, here is a sampling of courses listed in the Cornell University Courses of Study, 1987–88:

Communication
> Journalistic writing
> Professional writing
> Editing
> Writing for media
> Writing in the biological sciences

Arts and Sciences
>   Creative and expository writing
>   Narrative writing
>   Verse writing
>   The art of the essay

Institutions such as the University of Minnesota and Northwestern University have schools of journalism with extensive programs of study. Look and compare.

Top: Typewriters and word processors are very important tools for writers. (Dayton Daily News photo by Sol Smith)
Bottom: Writers must be able to tolerate long hours of working alone.

CHAPTER 3

IN THE BEGINNING

GETTING STARTED

Where?

A pleasant, well-lighted, and preferably soundproof room would seem to be the ideal place, preferably a room away from home where there can be no interruptions from family members, telephone callers, or the knocking of well-meaning friends.

John Hawkes said in an interview that he wrote one of his books "on a kind of paradise island in the West Indies," but he admitted to writing another "in the cab of a pickup truck in Montana."

Free-lance writers, especially those who write for magazines and newspapers, must be present in the milieu they are studying and cannot always afford to be too fastidious about their work place. Edward Mott Woolley, author of *Freelancing for Forty Magazines,* sometimes wrote in a Pullman berth "with my knees for a desk." Sherwood Anderson, being "not much of a desk man," wrote "anywhere and everywhere, usually on cheap yellow tablets ..." C. S. Forester wrote mostly in "free libraries," because "it was more comfortable there than in a cheerless, fireless room . . . although they are always full of shivering out-of-works . . ."

Travel writers may find themselves scribbling in a jet 36,000 feet up in the sky, while everyone else watches the movie.

Sometimes there is no choice. For example, I had to learn to read and write with fierce concentration while surrounded by three lively children, a television set, and a beagle.

When and How Long?

". . . mornings, afternoons, and evenings, and also during the night . . ."

C. S. Forester

The material for his first novels, Forester said, streamed down his arm and out of his fountain pen "in a torrent of six thousand words a day." He added that the work was "atrociously bad."

Each writer must determine his or her own best writing time. If there is a best time, it should be that time of day or night when your body energy is at its peak, for that is likely to be the time at which your mental energy is high, your mind at its clearest and quickest. Some people reach that peak during daylight hours; others come alive when most of the world is sleeping.

How long should you keep writing? Judging by the habits of established writers, the usual timespan lies somewhere between three and six or seven hours daily. Still, unless you are under the pressure of a deadline, rather than becoming a clockwatcher it might be preferable to set a reasonable minimum number of words, say five hundred to a thousand per day, no matter how long it may take. This frees you to concentrate on quality of work rather than quantity of time.

There is more than just writing time to be expended on your

business. There is "getting-down-to-work" time, for example. Ernest Hemingway used to spend an exceptional amount of time sharpening pencils. Other writers, upon approaching a typewriter, suddenly remember forgotten duties—walking the dog, watering the vegetable garden. Some simply cannot unleash their literary powers without one more cup of coffee. This is called procrastination, and since it doesn't count as writing time, shorten it as best you can.

There are also reading time, researching time, and interviewing time to be considered. These are less intense and demanding than actual writing time, but nonetheless time consuming.

Write!

Finally, the best way to get started is simply to get started. Sit down. Write or type something, even if it's only "I'd rather be hang-gliding." Write five hundred words right off the top of your mind. Write about your feelings about writing. Write about the curious pigeon eyeballing you from the cornice of a roof across the street. Write about the tree outside your window. Robert Frost did. "But tree, I have seen you taken and tossed/And if you have seen me when I slept,/You have seen me when I was taken and swept/And all but lost." The important word is *write,* and the answer to when is write now.

With What?

> "I cannot write more than three or four lines of longhand without fainting."
>
> James Thurber

Assuming you have a stand or desk to put it on, and a chair to sit on while you're using it, the typewriter is an indispensable tool. Buy, borrow, or rent, but get one. Whether you chop along with two fingers or can harness all ten, you will at some point for various reasons want to do your own typing. Some writers make technical and substantive changes right up to the final draft. Though you may prefer to do your daily stint by longhand, sooner or later a manuscript will have to be typed, and if your writing is covered with additions, emendations, and scratchings-out, as the pages pile up the typing job becomes a formidable one. It is highly heartening to confront a clear, clean copy.

Your Personal Library

The personal library you will want to accumulate ought to include such bare essentials as the following:

a handbook of literary terms
a good dictionary
Roget's Thesaurus
Strunk and White's *The Elements of Style*
The University of Chicago's *Chicago Manual of Style*
an up-to-date information almanac
a rhyming dictionary
Edith Hamilton's *Mythology*

You might also want to include some books by authors you admire, whose unique styles or descriptive powers stimulate your imagination. A subscription to a writer's craft magazine can offer practical help and marketing information.

What else do you need? Plenty of cheap paper and some 3 × 5 index cards. The latter are invaluable for research purposes and random jottings.

When it came to pens and penholders, Rudyard Kipling allowed himself to be eccentric. At various times he used a slim octagonal-sided agate penholder with a Waverly nib, a silver penholder with a quill-like curve, and an office-size pewter ink pot. As for you, if you are going to write by hand, determine your preferences in pencils or pens, stock up, and don't go out without one.

How to Survive

If, like the provident squirrel, you have a "nut" in the form of trust funds, savings, or inheritance money to nibble on during the hungry days, good for you. If not, you will have no alternative but to work part time or even full time while you build your writing business. No entrepreneur inaugurates a new business without capital set aside for initial investments and the red ink period.

THE HARDSHIPS

"Alone, alone, all, all alone
Alone on a wide, wide sea!"
from "The Ancient Mariner"
by S. T. Coleridge

Isolation—it's inevitable. There are times when writers absolutely must seclude themselves, must be able to tolerate long hours of working alone. Norman Jayo, a film director, producer, teacher, and scriptwriter had to leave his San Francisco apartment and lock himself in a motel room for a week in order to work with full concentration on a filmscript.

You cannot simply launch into a day's writing by sitting down and reading yesterday's last sentence, just as you cannot get out of harbor and go sailing without such essential preparations as raising and trimming the sail(s) and performing the other operations your vehicle requires. In writing, in order to plot the day's course you must have in mind a graphic vision of the beginning, the middle, and the end of the entire trip. All of this requires uninterrupted time. Plan for it.

Poverty

That albatross called poverty can be a heavy burden. During his days as an indigent beginner, C. S. Forester possessed but one pair of thin-soled shoes which sopped up winter's icy rains and sleets. With his first check he replaced them, and thereafter, whenever the postman brought a new check, he had an impulse to buy another and yet another pair of shoes. At last came financial security, and he exuberated, "I have a bank account which I have not overdrawn for eight years!"

Rejection

"I believe ... that genius ... is both much more common than we suppose and much more fragile."
Joyce Cary

By *genius* Cary meant *creative power.* And creative power often goes hand in hand with hypersensitivity. That brings us to rejection in the form of slips and slurs. Don't let your fragility shatter you. Be forewarned, and learn to control your sensitivity to the criticisms of others—well-meaning friends and family members, impersonal rejection slips. Don't let them discourage you. If you have a talent, you must believe in it and cultivate it, and it will flower. Think of Forester, who suffered the indignity of having his first three "immortal" novels returned via the postman all on the same day, and the added insult of having to remit postage on one of them!

"Writers have their own particular scars, thousands of them," free-lance writer E. M. Wooley wrote. He carried the "scar of the familiar editorial farewell, 'Very truly yours, The

Editors.' " Their anonymity, he felt, was grossly unfair; they should at least have signed their names!

Writing can be both emotionally and physically taxing. "I love my work with a love that is frenzied and perverted," Flaubert wrote, "as an ascetic loves the hair shirt that scratches his belly." Writing can be tormenting, wearying, tedious, and frustrating. Conversely, there are those moments which psychologist Abraham Maslow called "peak experiences" and which James Joyce described as "epiphanies," when we experience a sudden intuitive grasp of the reality and significance of some object or experience.

Some books write themselves. "I cannot say the book was written," Thomas Wolfe said in *The Story of a Novel.* "It was something that took hold of me and possessed me . . ."

Self-criticism

One more hazard—self-criticism. Not just fair, justified criticism meant to result in improvement, but debilitating self-criticism. You can never be perfect, and you may never be satisfied with what you write. If he could have done it all over again, William Faulkner told an interviewer, he would have done it better. What is required, he said, is "ninety-nine percent talent . . . ninety-nine percent discipline . . . ninety-nine percent work."

There are other hazards such as illness (yours or that of a member of your family), and family problems such as separations and divorces. And after publication, when you have established a name and are considered fair game, there may be bad press from reviewers and critics. All of these are hazardous factors in any occupation, and they will test the strength of your self-discipline. The July 1981 issue of *Writer's Digest* includes a special section entitled "How to Cope with the Stress of Writing." If you are subject to anxiety and feel you would like to learn more about handling the stresses of a writer's life, give the article a thoughtful reading.

Yes, writing can be overly stressful. But it can also be exciting, gratifying, enlightening, and profitable.

GETTING THE IDEA

"Dear old George Meredith the other day threw out an allusion (in something he was telling me) that suggested a small subject—5000 words . . ."

Henry James

"I have no special gift. I am only passionately curious."

Albert Einstein

James was always on the lookout for what he called "the precious article," the germ of an idea. To find the "precious article," you have only to look at and listen to the world around you with "passionate curiosity." If you do this, you will find yourself habitually summoning words to describe your perceptions—the particular pathos of a passing face, the slant of trees on a Sierra slope, the feeling of the mysterious emotional bond between a conductor and the symphony orchestra, the sound of rain on the waves of Cape Cod Bay. Let all your senses be receptive. Scents and textures are sometimes elusive—the smell of sun-warmed hair, the caress of a snow crystal.

Ideas? You will discover that you have them, perhaps in abundance. It may have been at least partly the prodding of your ideas that propelled you toward a writing career.

Ideas are everywhere, all the time—hidden in crannied walls, written across the sky. When you spot one, jot it down then and there in a little portable idea notebook or on 3 × 5 index cards, whether it's an idea for a digest filler or for plotting the world's greatest novel. Whatever it is, don't let it elude your memory. Catch it in all its pristine magnificence!

Suppose, for example, you are on a street in downtown San Francisco. You stop to listen to some street musicians, a violinist, a flutist, and a cellist, playing baroque music. You've seen such people before on the streets of Boston, on the campuses of California, playing every kind of music from renaissance to rock. Who are they? Where do they come from? What is their musical background? How much do they earn in this manner? Passers-by who pause to listen must certainly ask themselves such questions, so why not provide the answers in an article profiling selected street musicians?

At this point you reach for pencil and notebook.

Top: A film critic may work as a free-lancer or as a salaried member of a staff. (Dayton Daily News photo by Sol Smith)
Bottom: Editors frequently do some writing and almost always do much rewriting and editing. (photo by Carol Kim Retka)

CHAPTER 4

FREE-LANCE WRITING

Writers, like most other working people, fall into two categories: those who work for themselves, called entrepreneurs, and those who work for others, called employees. There are opportunities for writers in both categories. Such diverse writers as Walt Whitman, James Thurber, and Ernest Hemingway began in one category and crossed over to the other.

Suppose we take an overall view of the writing field in terms of potential jobs. Below is a list from the U.S. Labor Department's *Dictionary of Occupational Titles.* Some of these are free-lance jobs, some salaried, some could be one or the other. We will sort them out and look more closely at them later.

Columnist/Commentator	Continuity Writer
Copywriter	Screenwriter
Critic	Newscaster
Editorial Writer	Newswriter
Humorist	Reporter
Librettist	Script Reader
Lyricist	Copyreader
Playwright	Editor
Poet	Writer, Technical
Writer, Prose, Fiction,	Publications
and Nonfiction	

Along with the title of each job, the *Dictionary of Occupational Titles* provides a job description and designates the related media (press, radio, or books).

Suppose that after examining the above list you have made a decision to forego, temporarily, that great book you've been wanting to write. A book takes a solid chunk of time, and is usually rather difficult to sell, two factors which could be discouraging. Besides, you want more immediate earnings than a book could provide. In fact, you need them to strengthen your morale. So you have decided to try breaking into the free-lancer's market.

WHAT A FREE-LANCE WRITER ISN'T

The free-lance writer is not an employee. The free-lancer doesn't receive a salary and doesn't work full time in one particular place, such as an office, a factory, or a classroom. Therefore, though this writer may write for newspapers, magazines, book publishers, or all three, he or she is neither a staff news reporter nor a member of an editorial staff of a magazine or book publisher.

WHAT A FREE-LANCE WRITER IS

Free-lance writer . . . a writer who writes stories or articles for the open market with long-term commitments to no one publisher or periodical.
                    Webster's New Third International

The free-lance writer is an entrepreneur, running his or her own business. As such he or she must be a rigorous self-disciplinarian. If the person is a part-time professional writer, learning to apportion time will be vital. For example, an editor gives the green light on a story but specifies that it must be ready in three weeks. To accomplish this job the free-lance writer may find her or himself working long hours to meet that deadline and keep the editor's trust.

If the free-lancer is a novice, it is quite likely, as we have said, that in the beginning the person cannot survive on the earnings from his or her writing. Walt Whitman supported himself by working at a desk job in the Department of the Interior. For years Nathaniel Hawthorne was a customs clerk. Novelists often teach, give readings and lectures, and become writers-in-residence at educational institutions.

As for the free-lance writer's income from writing, it will be in the form of fees and royalties. The fees may be paid by the word or in a lump sum. Book publishers may (or may not) offer an advance, from which subsequent royalties will be deducted.

As an entrepreneur, the free-lance writer must choose his or her own work place, provide working tools, set a schedule, and pay his or her own expenses.

THE FREE-LANCE WRITER'S LIFE: A PROFILE

"You've got to love it," Norman Wilner told me during an interview in his San Francisco home. "It's very precarious, particularly in the beginning."

As a successful free-lance writer, instructor, humorist, and businessman, Norman Wilner knows well the meaning of the word *precarious.* Born in the slums of the Bronx in 1919, he attended public schools there, and at the age of nine won a fire prevention essay contest. "I wondered," he said, "where did this writing ability come from?"

During the depression he worked his way through City College, New York, and graduated with a bachelor's degree in social science.

He was well aware of his talent. "You have this power, but

how do you organize it?" Advertising, he thought, might be the answer.

"I started at the very bottom, with jobs like cleaning out the men's room. Worked my way up to copywriting."

And further. He became advertising manager of a large department store. He also began operating his own public relations agency.

"I was making $30,000," he said. "That was a lot of money in the forties. I could have made ten times as much, had I devoted myself full time to my business, but no, I had to write. Writing was my true love, and I'd have been a very unhappy man if I hadn't allotted time for my writing."

Norman Wilner is a natural humorist. He has a knack for composing what he called "funny, nutty, crazy, insulting letters. Groucho Marx-type letters." Actually, Groucho Marx read a collection of Wilner's letters and wrote him a fan letter, applauding his sense of humor. He began writing humorous restaurant news. Writing a newspaper column for a small magazine led to interviews and the sale of articles about a number of famous comedians.

Never give up. "I could paper the walls of my living room with rejection slips," Wilner said. "Save rejected articles and stories. Six months or a year later they may be saleable. After twenty-three rejections on a humorous article about Mel Brooks, I filed it away for future reference. A year later I sent it out again, and this time *TV News,* which had previously rejected it, liked it and bought it. You see? Never give up."

Esquire published his article on Zero Mostel, whom Wilner described as a "wild, hilarious, delightful guy." That led to another article, this one on Alan King, also published by *Esquire* and included in *Esquire's Anthology of Humor.* "*Esquire,*" he said, "gave me an entrée to other magazines."

When Wilner's wife once accused him of loving his typewriter more than he loved her, he agreed. "It's true. And furthermore," he told me, "your typewriter is a good substitute for a psychiatrist. It's great therapy, writing, and you save yourself $50 an hour!"

He advises his creative writing students not to write just for money. "For every million-dollar author there'll be a million starving writers out there . . ."

"I'm not wealthy," he told me. "But just think, with all the books William Faulkner wrote, he averaged only $600 a year from his writing. Just imagine. William Faulkner!"

"What other qualifications should a young writer possess?"

"Guts!" he emphasized. "Persistence. And faith in yourself."

Wilner has been working on a novel recently, and for seventeen years he has been teaching creative writing classes. I talked to him in September 1987, and he spoke of the gratification he feels when former students call or write to tell of their successes. "Eighty percent of my students haven't made it," he said, "simply because they haven't learned to put in at least an hour each day writing. But the other twenty percent—the 'slow and steady' group—by dint of writing and submitting their articles and stories with great persistence even in spite of multiple rejections—are gradually building a place for themselves in the writers' world."

A day in the life of one free-lance writer. "An average day? I wake up at 3 A.M. Put on the coffee. Admire my African violets. Sit down, work three or four hours by hand (it's quieter) until my wife wakes up. Then it's fresh coffee with her, and we chat a bit. Talk about our two kids. After that I work three or four more hours on the typewriter. Hard work, really. Just as hard as digging a ditch . . . very intense. I have a bit of lunch at 1 P.M., then a little nap. I work every day except Saturdays and Sundays and holidays. But I'm at it all the time.

Barefoot, taking a shower, making love, I'm always thinking writing. It's a happy obsession . . . like drugs without any ill effects. The years of experience count, too, you know. You're better at sixty-one than you were at forty-one. After the nap? I go on interviews, do research, go for a stroll, think about my work, whatever."

On moonlighting. "T. S. Eliot was a bank clerk, wrote poetry at night. Louis Auchincloss was a corporation lawyer. Sometimes it's necessary, especially at the beginning, to have a regular job during the week and do your writing mornings, evenings, and weekends."

That way, he said, free-lancing isn't so precarious.

CHAPTER 5

THE ESSAY/ARTICLE

"I Am Myself the Subject of My Book."
Michel de Montaigne

Now let us suppose that you have decided to become a free-lance writer, and not being ready to tackle a book, you have resolved to begin with an article. In our time an essay printed in a magazine or a newspaper is generally labeled an article. *Webster's New Collegiate Dictionary* defines the word *article* as referring to "a nonfictional prose composition usually forming an independent part of a publication (as a magazine)."

EARLY ARTICLES

The article is a descendant of the essay. For Michel de Montaigne, to *essai* meant to attempt, to test, or put to a trial. He did indeed put something to a trial over four hundred years ago. When he was forty-seven years old, he became the distinguished father of a new literary genre and a whole new division in literature: the essay. His first two books of *essais* were published in 1580.

"I want to be seen here in my simple, natural, ordinary fashion, without straining or artifice, for it is myself that I portray," he wrote. Montaigne believed that since all men have essentially the same basic human qualities, a deep subjective exploration of his own mind was, in effect, like holding a mirror to all mankind.

Francis Bacon's essays were published a few decades after Montaigne's. Unlike Montaigne's, they were objective, dry, and full of practical advice on social and political matters. For this reason he has been called the father of the formal essay.

The early essay was not closely associated with the news. But the coming of newspapers in the eighteenth century had a fundamental influence on the development and popularity of the essay in both form and content. In Addison and Steele's *Spectator* (initiated in 1711 and widely read and discussed in London), one found informality and humor along with criticisms of social foibles and failures. "The general purpose of this paper," Richard Steele wrote, "is to expose the false arts of life, to pull off the disguises of cunning, vanity, and affection, and to recommend general simplicity in our dress, our discourse, and our behavior."

The *Spectator* avoided both political and religious contention. But colonial newspapers in America became partisan in both religious and political affairs.

America counts among its many famed and favorite essayists Benjamin Franklin, Ralph Waldo Emerson, Henry David Thoreau, Oliver Wendell Holmes, James Russell Lowell, and Edgar Allan Poe. H. L. Mencken stands out in the early decades of the twentieth century. Among many others were Clarence Day, George Santayana, and James Thurber. The essay/article appears in all the media today. Radio and TV have condensed it into commentaries and "instant essays" such as those attributed to Eric Sevareid.

Let's suppose, finally, that you have decided to write about the aforementioned street musicians. But before beginning, to be sure no recent article or articles have been published on the subject, you visit a library reference room and search the *Readers' Guide to Periodical Literature,* covering the last five years. You find only one article, published in the *New Yorker,* and since your article is to be regional in its subject matter, you decide to go ahead.

ESSENTIALS OF A SUCCESSFUL ARTICLE

Style

Your article must be well written. The style must be fresh, not trite, and vivid, not dull. The word usage should be contemporary but free of jargon, except when quoting. Once you have decided where to send it, study the general style of the periodical you have chosen. The style that appeals to its editorial staff is the style you can assume to be attractive to its readers. Once you grasp the parameters of the general style, remember that the mode, the tone of expression, becomes a matter of your individual style.

Length

In general the length of an article should be commensurate with the dimensions of the idea or subject. If it is slanted toward a particular periodical, however, it should conform to that periodical's prescribed minimum/ maximum specifications.

If the article is too long, Mark Twain gave some advice: "One can seldom run his pen through an adjective without improving his manuscript."

Using many words where one word might do reveals that the writer has given up the search for *le mot juste,* the exactly right word. Padding dilutes your meaning and dulls the edge of your style. A good writer will quickly develop the skill of weeding out extraneous verbiage. What might require a paragraph of exposition can sometimes be said in one sentence of dialogue.

Timeliness

Your article should reflect current popular interests—or point to developing ones. Upton Sinclair in *Money Writes* cited an example of untimeliness. His article on Jack London, he said, was returned from a magazine edited by H. L. Mencken because the life of Jack London illustrated "the devastating effects of alcohol upon genius." What made the article untimely? At the time it was submitted, during Prohibition, the magazine was "committed to the policy of the 'return of the American saloon.' "

Succinctness

Your article must keep to the subject. However interesting they may be to the writer, digressions lose readers. Perhaps your digressions may be appropriate for another article. If so, cut and file them for future use.

Finally the work is completed. You've done your research (mostly live research, too, from primary sources, the best kind). You've interviewed a dozen or more groups of street musicians, sorted out the groups or individuals that seemed most interesting in terms of colorfulness, educational background, artistry, motivation, and life-style, and photographed and presented them in what you believe to be a lively and attractive style.

THE LITERARY MARKET

Now you must find the right publisher for your article. But where? Anthony Trollope gave his first manuscript to his mother. She got him a publisher and half the profits. But it doesn't usually work to rely on your mother. His mother was an exception—one of the popular novelists of her day.

So where do you begin your marketing project? Before we get down to specifics, perhaps this would be a useful point at which to take a look at today's literary market.

There are some dismal facts to be confronted when one is appraising the literary situation. To begin with, there were only about one hundred writers in the United States in 1976 who were making their living from their books, according to an estimate by John Leonard of the *New York Times.* In that same year over a third of P.E.N.'s membership, professional recognized writers in all genres, had not earned as much as $3,000. In 1978 the median income was $4,700. Based on that information it must be that hundreds of fine books go unpublished each year.

According to two New York editors in their book *How to Get Happily Published,* ninety percent of all manuscripts are turned down by commercial houses. To get published you must "crank out Top Forty material." So profit definitely crowds out quality. To survive, full-time writers today must write to sell. The writer must understand the vagaries of the market, must realize that with a few exceptions publishers do not lead, but follow, popular tastes.

Add to all this the conglomerization of the publishing industry, with a few large corporations controlling a great deal of the books published in the United States. Consolidation is the biggest recent happening in the book business. As an example, by the early eighties, big corporations like Gulf & Western, Raytheon Corporation, IBM, Litton, Exxon, ABC, and CBS, all with annual sales in the billions of dollars, had taken over from three to fourteen publishing companies each. Four of the conglomerates mentioned are listed in *The 100 Largest Defense Contractors,* and all of them are among the Fortune 500. Also, big publishers have been gobbling up smaller publishers, and newspapers and magazines such as the *Washington Post* and *Time* have done some swallowing, too.

Celeste West and Valerie Wheat, the authors of *The Passionate Perils of Publishing,* call this trend "conglomeritis" and "a dread disease of the land," but add that the independent, "alternative press" is "still alive, well, and doing better than ever." There has been, in fact, a national trade association of small publishers, called COSMEP.

Let's hope H. L. Mencken was right when he said "Literature thrives best in an atmosphere of hearty strife." Perhaps, though, Mencken would have found the present strife more disheartening than hearty.

How does this situation affect you, an up-and-coming freelance writer desiring to break into the magazine market?

CHAPTER 6

MARKETING YOUR ARTICLE

Free-lance writers hoping to be published must study to-day's specialized market. Each magazine has a posture, a slant, a point of view, or a set of beliefs. Each appeals to a particular class or category of readers. If you want a magazine to want what you write, write what it wants. The editors of *Powerboat Magazine* wouldn't stop the presses for an article on "Canoeing with Marquette and Joliet," or "Whitewater Rafting on Oregon's Roaring River."

WRITING FOR A MAGAZINE

A magazine, any dictionary will tell you, is a kind of ware-house, a place where goods and supplies are stored. In literary terms, a magazine or periodical is a collection of articles, stories, poems, and pictures directed either at a general reading public or at a special group sharing a hobby, profession, or interest.

Since Benjamin Franklin had a rather wide audience in mind when he conceived the idea of the first colonial magazine, he gave it an imposing title: *General Magazine and Historical Chronicle for All the British Plantations in America.* Printed in 1744, it missed being the first published magazine by three days. That Andrew Bradford's *American General*

Magazine appeared first was apparently due to skulduggery. Franklin's idea was stolen by one of his apprentices and his plans imparted to Bradford.

Periodicals grew rapidly in popularity. By the first quarter of the nineteenth century more than five hundred weeklies, monthlies, and quarterlies were being published. By 1890 there were nearly 3,000. The market continued to expand until television came along and claimed a share of the advertising market. Magazine publishers were afflicted by other problems, still prevalent today, such as rising costs of postage and of production.

But the magazine market, as you must have noticed, has expanded in many directions during the last couple of decades. For evidence, look inside the covers of *Writer's Market,* under such headings as "Consumer Publications," "Technical and Professional Journals," and "City." Many of the periodicals listed indicate what percentage of their articles are free-lance written. As a few random examples, in 1987, *Ebony Magazine* was buying ten manuscripts a year, *New Realities'* writers were twenty percent free-lance, and *Jack and Jill* was eighty-five percent free-lance. The range is from zero percent to one hundred percent.

The magazine market comprises a broad spectrum of opportunities for the free-lancer. Magazines have been classified in a number of different ways. Though they may overlap, I prefer the following groupings.

Mass Magazines	**News Magazines**
Ms.	*Newsweek*
TV Guide	*U.S. News and World*
Redbook	*Report*
Reader's Digest	

Class Magazines
Harpers
Saturday Review
New Republic
Atlantic

Specialized (Trade, Technical, and Professional) Magazines
Scientific American
Horse and Horseman
Bulletin of the Atomic Scientists
Fishing Tackle News

Business Publications
Marathon World
    (Marathon Oil Company)
The Enthusiast
    (Harley-Davidson)
Adventure Road
    (Citicorp Publishing)
Family Magazine
    (General Mills)

Little and Literary Magazines
Sewanee Review
Partisan Review
Poetry Magazine

To find a suitable market for your article, you decide to go to your local library. There the reference librarian directs you to the shelves where such resources as *LMP (Literary Market Place)* and *Writer's Market* are found. In one of these reference books you discover, under the heading "Article Markets" in the "City and Regional" section, just what you are looking for.

> *Westcoast Music.* 1750 Mozart Court, San Francisco, CA. Olivia Pickins, Editor. Published monthly. Interested in unusual features on all aspects of the performing arts. Mss. must be westcoast oriented, 500 to 2,500 words. Pays 10¢ a word on publication. Query.

Since your article is 2,500 words in length, if *Westcoast Music* magazine should buy it, you will have earned $250. If the manuscript should be returned, you have already made a second choice, which pays less and might require alterations.

You decide to query *Westcoast Music* magazine.

The Query Letter

What do you say in a query letter? Here is one composed by a very great author.

> Strictly speaking, the manuscript is not yet in a form to be submitted to you; nevertheless I venture to suggest that you should allow me to send you Part I, not, of course, for a decision or a promise of any kind, but only to give you a view of the subject and the treatment.
>
> If you would consent to look through it at your perfect leisure I would go on writing in the meantime . . .
>
> I would also, with the part 1st send you a short statement . . . of the idea . . . and this would enable you . . . to form an opinion as to whether I am going about it in a promising way—or otherwise . . .

The above was excerpted from a letter dated August 28, 1897, written by Joseph Conrad to Wm. Blackwood, publisher. Blackwood had already published some of Conrad's work, yet note how unassuming and tactful the letter is and how Conrad shies away from presumptuousness. Conrad's letter included the essentials of a query letter. Of course, one would probably not write such a letter today. For editors usually prefer a simple, direct query presenting the idea or subject of the work in one or two sentences, citing the author's background, previous publications if any, and special qualifications for the chosen subject. Your query might read as follows:

> Dear Ms. Pickins:
>
> I have just completed an article entitled "The Sound of Street Music" which I thought might be suitable for

Westcoast Music magazine. My article depicts the unusual life-style of California street musicians, their social and educational background, and their character. It explores their motivations, frustrations, and hopes for the future. I can submit a number of excellent photographs with my manuscript.

(Follow with your educational and professional background and qualifications, for example, editor of your high school literary magazine, reporter for your college daily newspaper, minor in music in college.)

Would you be interested in considering this article for *Westcoast Music* magazine?

Sincerely,

The Letter of Proposal

An alternative approach is to send a letter suggesting that you would like to do an article (or book) on a particular subject on which you have done research or in which you have had experience. In this case, you may wish to enclose an outline of the proposed work along with a brief sample—two or three typed pages for an article, a single chapter for a book.

The Final Appraisal

Before you put your manuscript in the mailbox, check it over one more time with the following questions:

- Is my article properly slanted to meet the needs of *Westcoast Music* magazine?
- Does it conform in style, subject, length, and slant to the magazine's specific requirements?
- Am I satisfied that my manuscript is sharply focused, vivid, and intriguing enough to hold the reader's interest?
- Is it in perfect shape—neat, unsmudged, clearly legible?

Have I double-checked it for typing errors, grammar, punctuation, and spelling?
- Are its paragraphs carefully composed units—one topic sentence each, clarified by related sentences?
- Is each paragraph linked logically and smoothly to its successor?
- If my manuscript is rejected, have I the confidence to continue my marketing search with another query letter, rewriting the article if necessary to fit new specifications?

If you can answer "yes" to these questions, "The Sound of Street Music" is ready for an editorial reading. Mail it.

ESTABLISHING A FREE-LANCE CAREER

When a full-time free-lancer stops working, he or she stops earning. Once a business-minded free-lance writer has posted the query letter, he or she will immediately begin work on another article, for the writer will need to have more than one or two manuscripts in the mail at all times. For the novice this may be an improbable achievement. The economic stress alone might be self-defeating. So again, a part-time job will serve to ease the writer into a free-lance career.

Should Ms. Pickins's response be a positive one, you will, in due time, become a published professional free-lance writer, and on publication you will have a title and a periodical name to refer to in ensuing queries. And hopefully, another and another. And not only the imaginary Ms. Pickins, but other real-life editors will begin to recognize your name as a qualified, reliable writer. From that point on it is plausible to begin asking to write "on assignment," in which case you need only query the editor on an idea, not a completed work. But for the time being you will be writing "on speculation," with no promises.

When you can produce articles of a style and literary quality suitable for the national magazine market, instead of $250 per article you may be earning $200 per page.

A popular novelist autographs books for her readers. (Scotland Yard Books, Ltd. photo by Betty Nicholas)

CHAPTER 7

THE NOVEL

> "She was the daughter of Zeus alone . . . Full-grown
> and in full armor, she sprang from his head."
> Edith Hamilton,
> *Mythology*

Great novels do not, as flashing-eyed Athena did, spring
from their authors' heads. It took James Joyce seven years
to complete *Ulysses*. Virginia Woolf worked on *The Waves*
for two years, and when told it was a masterpiece, she
wrote, "Now for a cigarette and then a return to sober composition . . ."

Listen to the comments of some noted writers on various
aspects of the craft of writing.

Edgar Allan Poe on plotting:

> "Nothing is more clear than that every plot, worth the
> name, must be elaborated to its denouement before
> anything be attempted with the pen."

Robert Louis Stevenson on technique:

> ". . . the just and dexterous use of what qualities we
> have, the Proportion of one part to another, and to the
> whole, the elision of the useless, the accentuation of the
> important, and the preservation of a uniform character
> from end to end . . . These, taken together, constitute
> technical perfection."

James Branch Cabell on rewriting:

> "My first drafts are handwritten and then typed with dejection and many changes."

Saul Bellow on art vs. virtuosity:

> ". . . you have only to listen to Paganini and then to Mozart to realize the difference between the virtuoso and the artist."

Longinus on word usage:

> "The use of trivial words is very apt to disfigure great passages."

GENESIS OF THE GENRE

Fiction is as old as civilization. Stories of magic written in Egypt on papyrus four thousand years ago still survive, as do beast fables, fairy tales, fabulous tales like the *Arabian Nights,* and epics such as Homer's *Iliad* and *Odyssey.* We still enjoy the medieval romances, those long epic stories of the adventures of such heroes as King Arthur and Charlemagne.

The prehistory of the novel spanned many centuries. But the modern novel as we know it today emerged during the eighteenth century in the words of such diverse writers of narrative fiction as Samuel Richardson, Henry Fielding, and Aphra Behn in England; Voltaire, Rousseau, Madame de La Fayette, and Denis Diderot in France.

The novel reached its highest development during the nineteenth century with Balzac and Flaubert in France; Dostoevski, Tolstoy, Turgenev, and Gogol in Russia; Sir Walter Scott, Jane Austen, Charles Dickens, William Makepeace Thackeray, and Thomas Hardy in England; and, in America, James Fenimore Cooper, Nathaniel Hawthorne,

Herman Melville, Henry James, Mark Twain, and William Dean Howells.

Firsts: American and English

"I cannot live without you and since the thing has gone so far I will not!" And so he clasped me in his arms, in such a manner as quite frightened me; and kissed me two or three times . . . I got from him and ran up stairs, and went to the closet . . ."

Samuel Richardson's book, *Pamela: or Virtue Rewarded,* originally intended to be a book of letters to be used as models, became not only one of the eighteenth century's best sellers, but the first dramatic novel.

Poor Pamela is abducted and imprisoned by her bachelor-master, but through it all—the prurient attractions and repulsions, the repeated threats by Mr. B to her prized bourgeois virtue—she survives unviolated and finally marries Mr. B, who is no longer a libertine, but a man claiming to have "conquered" his "more culpable passions" and become the victim of Pamela's virtue. *Pamela* was the first offspring of the alleged originator of the modern novel, Samuel Richardson.

The first published American novel, with the portentous and edifying title *The Power of Sympathy or The Triumph of Nature Founded in Truth,* was actually a tale of scandal and seduction. Authorship was attributed to a woman, Sarah Wentworth Apthorp Morton of Boston. But the actual author is said to have been William Hill Brown, who lived across the street from Sarah Morton. Brown, so it is said, based parts of his sentimental and didactic book on allegedly scandalous affairs going on across the street in the Morton manse. The Mortons later tried to buy and destroy all copies, but one was found in an old trunk and the tale of seduction survives.

The creator of *Pamela* had a printing business. But the man known as the first professional novelist, Charles Brockden Brown, an American, sought a full-time career in literature when no such career existed. His first novel, *Wieland,* was published in 1798. Within three years he had written five more, all dealing with philosophic and moral problems, but gothic in tone and often involving crime, romance, and marriage.

Financially, Charles Brockden Brown failed. No professional American writer before Washington Irving succeeded. The profession truly began with Cooper and Irving in the early nineteenth century. And at the middle of that century it had reached great heights.

First Novels Today

So *Pamela,* let's say, was the very first *first* novel. And Brown's *Wieland* was the first *first* novel by an American. According to *Publishers Weekly,* in the fall of 1980 over one hundred first novels were listed by major United States publishing houses. Since then the figure has gone up and down, but according to the *Library Journal,* March 15, 1987, "A record-breaking 182 novels, from 47 publishers, make up the new harvest of first fiction this season." Below are excerpts from comments made by a few of these novelists.

Michael F. Anderson, author of *The Unholy:*

> ". . . sometimes you have to get hurt before you win.
> When you go down in round one, you get up and fight
> on. Or you quit. Everyone has the choice."

Donna Levin, author of *Extraordinary Means:*

> "I hope for recognition for what I do, but no amount of recognition will be enough if I can't enjoy the daily process . . ."

Michael Allegretto, author of *Death On the Rocks:*

> "I didn't feel that I was *lucky* to be published, or even that I *deserved* to be published, but rather that I had *learned how* to be published. And it felt great."

It requires about 40,000 copies to make a best-seller. Sometimes a first novel, to the writer's amazement, can rise to become a best-seller. A first novel may even become a good and profitable movie. Sometimes publishers pay fabulous prices for new novels, even for first novels. These are rare exceptions; publishers don't gamble. For example, in the fall of 1987 Warner Books paid $750,000 for world English-language rights to *Promises to Keep,* a roman à clef about the Kennedy assassination by George Bernau. Yes, it was Bernau's first novel. But he is a lawyer and an excellent researcher who had been pondering the tragic death of Kennedy for some twenty years. Furthermore, as a motion picture lawyer, he must have acquired considerable expertise in the legal and other aspects of authoring and marketing fiction.

According to the June 5, 1981, issue of *Publishers Weekly,* ". . . studio executives and independent producers in Hollywood . . . prefer full-length books over original screenplays." Why? We can assume it is for the good plots and fleshed-out characters which provide directors, actors, and writers with an in-depth concept of their "movie-to-be."

Books most often chosen for film adaptation are usually either best-sellers and literary classics, or unknown titles, first novels, and other books that adapters can alter to their own specifications.

MARKETING YOUR FIRST NOVEL

The Role of the Agent

Most of today's editors haven't the time to read over-the-transom material.

Get an agent if you can. Agents, unfortunately, are far from anxious to represent unpublished writers. The reason is obvious. Most prospering agents have an established clientele from whom they can count on their usual ten to fifteen percent commission. Newcomers are a gamble. If you decide to try to find an agent, one place to look is in *Literary Market Place*. It contains an extensive list of active authors' agents.

Good agents are skilled at matching books and publishers. An agent can save you from those depressing rejection slip blues. Instead, you can turn your back on the mailbox and funnel your energy into another manuscript while the previous one is being considered. After finding an appropriate publisher, the agent will use his or her expertise to negotiate contracts and rights with the publisher. The standard agent's fee is ten percent. If you can find the right agent, it is well worth it.

The Writer's Guild of America East Newsletter of April 1980, carried some writers' comments on agents.

"Never sign with an agent who you feel is doing you a favor," George Malko wrote.

"The arrogance of many agents, especially toward new writers," according to Harvey Jacobs, "is not only shocking, it's ludicrous."

And Alan Seeger observed that writers "always seem to want the agent who is representing someone else."

The authors also offered some suggestions:

- Most agents will not read unsolicited manuscripts.
- Unless you include a self-addressed, stamped envelope, most agents will not read your query letter.

- Sending out multiple queries to agents is acceptable. Sending a manuscript to two agents at a time is not.
- Don't let yourself get discouraged if an agent turns you down; just seek another.
- Finally, before you submit your manuscript to an agent, make sure that it is polished to a sparkle and that you are convinced it is publishable. If an agent agrees to handle it, be clear about his or her commission, any other fees, and the terms of the agreement or contract, if any.

Some Revealing Statistics

The statistics below, published in *Publishers Weekly,* apply to writers of books. Keep in mind as you study them that they include both fiction and nonfiction books.

In 1979 Columbia University's Center for the Social Sciences conducted a survey of the financial situation of 2,239 authors. The study was made for the Authors Guild Foundation. According to Peter S. Prescott, Authors Guild Foundation president, the findings should serve to correct the widespread publicity accorded a few million-dollar best-sellers, the effect of which "has given the public a false and distorted picture of how American authors live."

In this survey a writer was defined as "one who had at least one book published," according to *Publishers Weekly*'s Madalynne Reuter. In fact, half of the writers who responded had had four books published.

Nearly half of those queried worked at other jobs besides free-lance writing.

University teaching	36%
Other professional occupations	20%
Publishing industry	11%
Journalism	5%
Public relations	5%

School teaching 4%
A variety of occupations .15%
Full-time authors 5%

The truth appears to be that "most book authors can't . . . make ends meet from their writing alone." Half of the survey's participants earned less than $5,000 in 1979 "from writing and writing-related activities." The median income was $4,775. Twenty-five percent of the writers earned less than $1,000. Ten percent earned above $45,000.

And what was the primary type of writing done by these authors?

Adult nonfiction 26%
General adult fiction 20%
Children's books 15%
Genre fiction 13%
Academically oriented nonfiction 12%
How-to books 6%
Technical reports, manuals, textbooks 3%
Poetry 2%
Religious-inspirational 1%
Other 2%

The study indicated that race and educational attainment were not factors in a writer's financial success, although gender was. Women writers earned a median of $4,000, whereas the median for men was $5,000.

It is true that every now and then a million-dollar best-seller comes along. Very rarely is it a first novel by a newcomer in the writing profession. A writer who sets out deliberately to write a best-seller may be blinded by the dollar signs in his or her eyes.

ABOUT SELF-PUBLISHING

Dorothy Bryant's novels grace bookstore and library shelves all across the United States. She taught school for years before she began writing. "My role models were teachers, not writers," she told me. In the following interview, she explains how self-publishing works, and points out its advantages and disadvantages. Bryant comments, "When I began writing, I went to San Francisco State University to get an M.A., not because I thought an advanced degree in writing was essential, but because it was a way of getting into college teaching, where I would have more flexibility."

Q. *What was the title of your first novel?*

A. *Ella Price's Journal.* It took me four years to find a publisher. Lippincott published it in 1972.

Q. *And the very popular second novel?*

A. *The Kin of Ata Are Waiting for You.* It was originally a self-published book, until Random House finally picked it up.

Q. *And it became known as a "cult" book?*

A. Yes. The publishing industry is reluctant to acknowledge that a book they didn't bet on will somehow sell. If it does, despite lack of promotion and no reviewing, they call it a "cult book." It's been in print now for ten years, selling quite steadily, and there's always a movie option on it. The publishers didn't want my third book, *Miss Giardino.* It had made the rounds of New York publishers for about six years. It's harder to get a third book published. Today the publishers want instant success; they aren't willing to invest in the future product of a talented writer. So I thought, well, I will just publish my books myself! A very naive decision, considering the many problems and frustrations about which I knew very little. If I'd been aware of them, I probably wouldn't have gone ahead and done it!

Q. Would you recommend self-publishing for others?

A. Though it has worked out fairly well for me, I'm not recommending it; I'm not saying self-publication is the answer. In fact, I don't think there is any answer for anyone in the arts. You are not going to make money unless you are one of the top three percent, you know. So if you don't love to write, you might as well not do it.

Q. How do you feel about vanity publishing?

A. That's not for me. You are paying someone to print your book and supposedly to publish it. They will charge you a lot of money up front, and they haven't put any money into it and almost no editing. Anyone who writes to a publisher who proposes to publish your book for a fee will get back a letter saying, "Oh, this is great!" They promise to print the book and send out review copies, and maybe they do, but when the newspapers and magazines see the name of the publisher, they recognize it as a paid vanity publisher, and they throw the book out. No, I wouldn't recommend vanity publishing.

Q. How do you go about the business of publishing your own books?

A. The work splits into two parts: production and sales. In producing the book I have editors—paid and unpaid, mostly unpaid friends—who go over my work and give me suggestions. I hire a local typesetter. I do the paste-up myself. These are very expensive processes, and because I must keep the costs down, I do everything but the copyediting. I always hire a proofreader because you just can't catch all the errors in your own words. The book is typeset here and a camera-ready copy is sent to a printer in Ann Arbor, Michigan, a center for small press printing that charges less and does a better job than here.

Q. So how do you arrive at a price for your books?

A. You have to charge at least five times your production cost. A lot of self-publishers don't understand this; consequently they go broke and into debt. The bookstores take forty percent, the distributors another fifteen percent. By the time you whittle off all your costs, you are down to very little return. I do a printing of about three thousand, and I store the books in my basement. Most of them are distributed through wholesalers. So that is the way the self-publishing business works.

Q. What do the statistics tell us about free-lance writers' incomes?

A. In this country they earn less than $5000 a year. The other three percent—the ones you read about in the newspapers—are a tiny proportion. There are angry, bitter people out there who have aspired to make big money in writing, but it's like playing the slot machines. If my only objective was to hit the jackpot, I'd probably quit, because there are easier ways to make money.

Q. How is the aspiring new writer to survive?

A. By working at another job. A compatible job. Take nursing, for example. A nurse can go anywhere in the world, work any hours, and is in touch with people in extreme and dramatic situations. Find some profession that works with your writing.

Q. I suppose people ask, are you able to make a living as a writer?

A. I do about as well as the average writer. And through self-publishing I have control over the distribution of my books. That's important! If commercially published books don't become best-sellers, their shelf-life is very short. They go out of print, and after six months there's nothing out there. That makes writers very unhappy. And that can't happen to me.

Dorothy Bryant earns half the family income, her husband the other half. "I'm not complaining," she told me. "It's a good life."

CHAPTER 8

THE SHORT STORY

"I like the fiction writer's feeling of being able to confront an experience and resolve it as art."

Eudora Welty

"A good story is an intelligible and lasting shape carved out of time."

Malcolm Cowley

A short story might be thought of as a portrait miniature such as those which flourished from the sixteenth to the nineteenth century. The miniatures were so tiny that they could be enclosed in lockets or tiny portrait boxes, yet some were so finely painted that when seen through a magnifying glass they retained their vividness and clarity. Like the miniature, the short story demands dramatic intensity, subtlety, and finesse.

THE MASTERS

Beginning short story writers would benefit from reading the masters: Guy de Maupassant for his realism and irony; Anton Chekhov for his deep and compassionate understanding of human nature; O. Henry for his surprising denouements; Edgar Allan Poe for his psychological acumen and his skill at suspense building; Hawthorne for his structure, style,

57

and symbolism. Others to be studied are Nicolai Gogol, Henry James, Mark Twain, Rudyard Kipling, James Joyce, Ernest Hemingway, William Faulkner, Sherwood Anderson, Thomas Mann, Franz Kafka, Flannery O'Connor, and Eudora Welty.

The nineteenth century, a time of experimentation with new forms, was the time of the flowering of the short story both in America and in Europe. "Rip Van Winkle" is considered to be the first American short story.

As the short story evolved, two schools of thought emerged. Edgar Allan Poe formulated the principle of the single effect around which the unity of the story was to be built. But in Russia, Turgenev advanced the theory that revelation of character was the focal point of the story. Some writers were attracted to the idea of the primacy of plotting, others to character illumination, an artificial separation, which is, in effect, negated by their being as inextricably intertwined as the double helix.

THE MARKET

The short story, often considered a stepping-stone along the path to the novel, is a literary genre in its own right.

"We have been told that the novel is dead, and I am sure that someone has said as much for the short story," Frank O'Connor said in *The Lonely Voice.* O'Connor went on to say that he thought the announcement "premature."

In his contribution to a symposium organized by the *Kenyon Review* between 1968 and 1970, William Saroyan wrote, ". . . the bottom has dropped out of the short story market." The fault, he said, was with the writers. And if the short story was to make a comeback it was the writers who would have to make it happen.

That the economic state of the short story had definitely

declined seems to have been the consensus of the thirty writers from around the world who participated in the symposium. Most all of them praised the short story as an artistic form, but agreed that it was not possible, as it was in the days of O. Henry, to live on one's earnings from short story writing.

Although the paying market for short stories may not be in the best of health, the short story is a long way from expiring. And who is to say that it will not flourish and even become a lucrative literary form once again? There is evidence that this may be happening.

An editorial in the winter 1981 *Antioch Review* reported, "There is a boom in short story writing in this country and its significance has escaped notice." During 1980, *Antioch Review* received 1,925 short stories. All were given a reading. But less than one percent appeared in *Antioch Review*'s pages.

"The rejection rate is astounding," the editorial said, and it claimed that this publication was receiving an "outlandish number of excellent stories." The publication of more short story collections and the praise given in reviews and interviews to seasoned writers like Eudora Welty, and more recently to younger writers like Bobbie Ann Mason, appear to be promising signs.

The *Writer* published a list of little, literary, and college magazines in its March 1987 issue. It is only a partial list; there are many, many more magazines whose editors are seeking stories by talented writers. The *International Directory of Little Magazines and Small Presses,* published annually and very likely available in the reference division of your public library, presents a complete list of such magazines. Below is a random sampling:

Black Maria—P.O. Box 25187, Chicago, IL 60625. Feminist. Short stories and experimental fiction, to 3,500 words. Poetry of any form. Articles; essays; B&W photos, graphics. Pays in copies.

The Chariton Review—Northeast Missouri State Univ., Kirksville, MO 63501. Jim Barnes, Ed. Highest quality poetry and fiction, to 6,000 words. Modern and contemporary translations. Book reviews. Pays $5 per printed page for fiction and translations.

The Long Story—11 Kingston St., N. Andover, MA 01845. Stories, 8,000 to 20,000 words; prefer committed fiction. Pays $1 a page, on publication. Poetry.

Michigan Quarterly Review—3032 Rackhan Bldg., Univ. of Michigan, Ann Arbor, MI 48109. Laurence Goldstein, Ed. Scholarly essays on all subjects; fiction; poetry. Pays $8 a page, on publication. Annual contest.

Mind in Motion—P.O. Box 1118, Apple Valley, CA 92307. Celeste Goyer, Ed. Fiction, 500 to 2,500 words: allegory, fable, surrealism, parody; poetry, to 45 lines: emphasis on universal concerns artfully directed toward everyday and esoteric. Pays in copies.

New Letters—5216 Rockhill Rd., Kansas City, MO 64110. James McKinley, Ed. Fiction, 10 to 25 pages; nonfiction, 20 to 30 pages. Poetry; submit 3 to 6 at a time.

Nycticorax—P.O. Box 8444, Asheville, NC 28814. John A. Youril, Ed. Short-short fiction and poetry (submit 4 to 8 poems at a time). Query about essays on literary criticism. Pays in copies.

Piedmont Literary Review—P.O. Box 3656, Danville, VA 24543. Fiction, to 4,000 words. Poems, of any length and style. Special interest in young poets. Pays in copies. Submit up to 5 poems.

There is a market for short stories among general interest magazines such as *Commentary, Capper's Weekly, Collage,* and *Women.* However, the short story market among general interest magazines is sharply competitive. There may be multiple rejections before a sale.

On the other hand, among little or literary magazines and reviews there is always a demand. They want to see quality fiction, and publication, if not profitable, is prestigious and counts with other editors. Be sure your submission fits within the scope of a magazine by first studying several current issues.

You can find more markets for short stories in the *Writer's Market,* listed under such headings as "Health and Fitness," "Juveniles," "Lifestyles," "Music," "Teens," "Science Fiction," and "Romance and Confession."

Suggested Reading

Foley, Martha, ed. *Two Hundred Years of Great American Short Stories.* New York: McMillan, 1972.

King, Woodie, comp. *Black Short Story Anthology.* New York: Columbia University Press, 1972.

May, Charles E., ed. *Short Story Theories.* Athens: Ohio University Press, 1978.

Menton, Seymour, comp. *The Spanish-American Short Story.* Los Angeles: UCLA Latin American Center Publications.

Authors are often asked to lecture on their areas of expertise.
(University of Iowa photo)

CHAPTER 9

NONFICTION BOOKS

"Every nonfiction writer carries dozens of half-formed
book ideas in his head at once. You need only let them
mature at their own pace."

John Gunther

As anyone can see by strolling inside a bookstore, a very
high percentage of books published today falls into the nonfiction category.

CATEGORIES

Categorizing nonfiction books is a tempting but difficult
project, perhaps because like the person who writes it, each
book is unique. In *Writing a Non-Fiction Book,* author John
Gunther suggests the following classifications:

the adult how-to book
the alarmer or exposé
the microcosmic adventure
   narrative
the current narrative

the historical narrative
the biography or ghosted
   autobiography
the anthology

DEFINITIONS AND APPROACHES

For our purposes we will look at the how-to book, the descriptive book, the exposé, the narrative, and the biography.

The How-To Book

Nobody can write an authoritative how-to book on any subject without sound personal knowledge of that subject. Suppose you want to write a book about fishing, for example. There are probably thousands of books in print on the subject of fishing. How then are you to hook a publisher? What lure should you use?

Isaac Walton knew the subject, and his book *The Compleat Angler,* published in 1653, had five editions in twenty-three years. The book is full of philosophical comments, quotations from poetry, and delightful rambling conversation about the customs and opinions of Walton's day, not to mention "innocent harmless mirth in several places mixed," as Walton put it, so that the book might not "read dull and tediously." He suggested that if the reader disliked the book, he might like "the excellent pictures of the trout, and some of the other fish."

A good how-to book should never "read dull and tediously." Its unique style and recurrent flashes of humor, both stemming from the personality of its author, should concurrently entertain and instruct the reader.

Good Dog, Bad Dog, as you might expect, is a book on how to train a dog. It begins with housebreaking, works its way through "sit" and "sit-stay" to "After the Obedience Course" and finishes with "The Breeds, A Dictionary of Training." What's different about this book? "Equal emphasis is given to teaching the owner as well as the animal," the authors tell us in the introduction.

Good Dog, Bad Dog is an instructive book. It could have been more entertaining, too, with a touch of humor here and there.

There is a good market for how-to books today. Meander around a bookstore for the evidence, and you will see books on careers, hobbies, arts and crafts; books on how to make money, how to hypnotize yourself, how to fall in love, how to fall out of love, how to choose a psychiatrist, how to break off with your psychiatrist, how to win at the race track, and how to write nonfiction. No matter that there are numerous books on your chosen subject already in print. All you need is a new angle, a fresh approach. If you are qualified and want to write one, leaf through some successful how-to's in your library or local bookstore. Examine the tables of contents, the arrangements of the chapters. Read enough to get the general tone, the feel of the book. A how-to book should be easy, even fun, to read. It should clarify, not confuse. It should instruct without lecturing or "writing down" to the reader. Put the best facets of your own personality into your how-to book. Isaac Walton did, with more than modest success.

The Descriptive Book

The descriptive book explores a subject, but stops short of instructing. It explains or illuminates. *Time* magazine called the book *The Poverty of Power* "a closely reasoned, adult primer on energy." The *Chicago Daily News* said that it was "a monumentally important contribution to public debate . . ." Even though the author, Barry Commoner, takes a specific stand on energy and the economic crisis, the book is not polemical. It is designed not to harangue, but to enlighten through a calm, logical description of the energy situation as Commoner sees it.

The First Three Minutes by Stephen Weinberg describes the cosmic events believed by some astrophysicists to have taken place during the first three minutes following the big bang, when the cosmos was born.

If you were to write a book entitled *My Visit to Afghanistan* or a book called *Corn Country* about life on a farm in Iowa, you would be writing descriptive books. The immediacy of *My Visit to Afghanistan* (even with such a poor title) might attract an audience. We're curious about this rugged Asian country, particularly in view of Soviet-American relations and the involvement of both the Soviet Union and the United States in military and political affairs there. But *Corn Country*?

The fact that you happen to have grown up on an Iowa farm, and you know the territory and the people like the back of your well-weathered hand doesn't necessarily make the subject interesting. But suppose that at the center of that area stands a church, which, as the focal point of a curiously fascinating religious sect, has had, to your certain knowledge, a major and critical influence over the life-styles of hundreds of Iowan farmers and their families. That would be something which might appeal to a large readership and therefore also to editors and publishers. If *Corn Country* merely described the history of this church and told the story of the growth and influence of the sect, it would be a descriptive book. Even if the sect induced its members to indulge in some sort of sinister behavior which you documented and presented in the form of case histories, as long as you do not take a heated position or urge an investigation, your book remains a descriptive one.

The Exposé

The difference between a descriptive book and an actual exposé lies in their respective purposes. The usual intent in an exposé is to discredit or alarm in order to correct. It is easy to recognize an exposé book, if not by its title, then by its chapter headings.

Cry of the People by Penny Lernoux, published by Doubleday in 1980, is dedicated "to the poor people of Latin America."

Parts of the table of contents read as follows:

> Chapter 1: Torture—The Rise of Fascism—The Agony of the Church.
>
> Chapter 2: Repression—The Recognition of Human Rights.

Cry of the People is obviously an exposé. The author, avowedly, is writing about "the Catholic Church's struggle against military dictatorship in Latin America," as she announces in the introduction; her work is solidly documented, and she discredits the governments responsible for the actions she exposes for public readership.

Another exposé, *Male Practice: How Doctors Manipulate Women,* by Robert S. Mendelsohn, M.D., states on its dust jacket, "If you are a woman living in America the greatest danger to your health is, in all likelihood, your own doctor." Dr. Mendelsohn's chapter headings quote manipulative doctors.

> Chapter 8: "I'm Afraid We'll Have to Operate."
>
> Chapter 9: "What Do You Need a Uterus for, Anyway?"

Dr. Mendelsohn, formerly national director of Project Head Start's medical consultation service and chairman of the medical licensing committee for the state of Illinois, has received recognition in the form of many awards for excellence in medicine and medical instruction. He draws upon a sure knowledge of his subject, carefully documents the facts he cites, and calls upon women readers to be alert to the dangers of the subject.

If you plan to write an exposé, be sure that among your

qualifications are genuine expertise on the subject and a vital interest in it.

Presumably a roman à clef might be considered an exposé, since it reveals the usually secret side of the lives of real people described in disguise as fictional characters, but recognizable nonetheless. But it ought not to be called an exposé if it merely appeals to nosy or prurient-minded interests in people.

The Narrative

An account of a series of events, the narrative may be either contemporary or historical, or perhaps both. And (to illustrate the difficulties of classification) what are we to call Francis Parkman's *Oregon Trail*? A Harvard University graduate with a love of natural beauty and authentic literary skill, Parkman became one of America's great historians. His journey across the Great Plains, begun in 1846 and recorded in his book *The Oregon Trail,* was an exciting adventure story and a descriptive narrative with some current history blended in.

Suppose you had in mind writing a book about Eugene Debs and his quest for the presidency of the United States. Debs ran for president as the Socialist party candidate (a political party which he led in establishing) in 1900, 1904, 1908, and 1912, and then again in 1920, when he received 920,000 votes while in prison for criticizing government prosecution of persons charged with violating the 1917 Espionage Act. This book could be a historical narrative.

If you went rock climbing in the Himalayas and lived to write about it, your book would very likely be a descriptive narrative. If you went to interview a guerilla group opposing a South American dictator and were arrested by the dictator's military police and held and tortured for refusing to name names, the story of your experience would be turned into an exciting, harrowing adventure narrative. It might be an exciting adventure and nothing more, or, depending upon the depth of the knowledge, analysis, and writing of the experience, it might have illuminating social or philosophical overtones.

Writing Biography

It isn't imperative that you be a doctor of philosophy in literature (or in anything else) to write a credible and creative biography. But biographical writing requires a great deal of skilled research and reading, interviewing, and perhaps considerable traveling. Your subject may have moved from city to city, or even from country to country, leaving behind important records and intimate friends, colleagues, and business associates. There is a detailed chronology of events in the subject's life to be assembled. And one must remember that a human life is more than a chronicle of events or successes and failures and that the whole must transcend the sum of all the parts. Toward that end the biographer brings to bear imagination, insight, and self-understanding, for if you have no more than a superficial concept of your own character, you cannot yet hope to reach any great depth of mature human understanding as a biographer.

A biography need not be impersonal and heavily data-laden. A keen, subtle insight into human nature will enable the biographer to see through the periphery of dates and data to the heart of the life story, to what he or she conceives to be its central idea, organizing principle, or motivating force. Around this center the writer will build the organic structure of the biography, being scrupulously careful not to compromise faithfulness to truth by distorting facts to conform to his or her idea.

Is there a market for biographical writing? Emphatically yes. Beginning biographers are not apt to have the opportunity to write about very famous living persons. Such books are usually composed by seasoned professionals.

For a historical biography, check the material in print. A new biography of a historical personage will be welcomed if its approach is fresh and its appeal timely.

Nancy Milford's book *Zelda* seems to have been a labor of love, for Milford spent six years researching and writing this biography, and in the process she interviewed more than one hundred people. She had long been fascinated by the arresting personalities of Scott and Zelda Fitzgerald and began, at age twenty-five, to "gather reminiscences" from the couple's friends and acquaintances. In 1963 she traveled from New York to Baltimore and Washington, "into the Smoky Mountains to Asheville, and then down deeper through the heat and pines of Georgia to Montgomery, Alabama, in search of Zelda." Her search for Zelda took her to London, Paris, and Switzerland.

The books on the biography shelves in a good college or university library will provide direction for anyone considering writing a biography. Some universities will issue you a library card (perhaps for a fee) to use while you are writing your book. The number of reference books on biography will surprise you.

If your subject is a living person, try *Current Biography* and the *Dictionary of International Biography, Who's Who in America, Who's Who in the Midwest*—or whatever regional *Who's Who* you require.

If your subject is no longer living, there is *Who Was Who in America,* and *Notable American Women, 1607–1950.*

There are also reference works based on profession or occupation, such as the *Concise Biographical Dictionary of Singers, American Men and Women of Science, International*

Encyclopedia of Film, and *Who's Who in American Politics.*
There are literally hundreds of titles available, but of course
not all your research can be done in a library, as Nancy
Milford's odyssey illustrates.

Biographical writing demands expert researching skills,
objectivity, loyalty to the truth, and plenty of time. In choosing his or her subject, the biographer ought to be certain of
the ultimate public value of the book and of the worthiness of
the purpose in writing it.

Interviewers ought to have a strong interest in the people they select to interview. (Dayton Daily News photo by Sol Smith)

CHAPTER 10

WRITING REVIEWS AND INTERVIEWS

BOOK REVIEWS

"Truly major critics have an influence that transcends the power of any periodical in which their writing appears."

Richard Kostelanetz

There is certainly no shortage of books, nor even of books that merit reviewing. Billions of dollars worth of books are sold each year. But not all books, and certainly not all meritorious books, are reviewed. Much depends upon promotion by the publishers.

Book reviews come in two general categories: the journalistic or short review, and the essay review. The scope of the short review is limited to a description of the book's contents in a few short paragraphs along with the reviewer's reaction to and opinion of its value. You will find examples of the short review in newspapers, Sunday supplements, and news magazines.

The essay review is longer, more detailed, and more comprehensive and is found in publications such as the *New York Review of Books,* the *New York Times Book Review,* and the *Times Literary Supplement.*

There are some five specialties among professional critics: book critics, art critics, drama critics, movie critics, and music critics.

A critic is an established reviewer who has distinguished her or himself to such an extent that personality, judgment, and understanding alone will attract an audience. The sharp, original, and controversial opinions of certain critics create a magnetic appeal. H. L. Mencken, to whom no subject was sacred, was one of these. Commenting on Warren Harding's inauguration address, he wrote: "It was so bad that a kind of grandeur crept into it."

A germane sentence appears in John Drewry's book, *Writing Book Reviews:* ". . . the more one brings to the task of reading and reviewing by way of personal erudition, understanding, and discrimination, the better job he can do." Drewry is talking about cultural background, about a good formal education, about a long and broad acquaintanceship with books, and familiarity with the media—daily newspapers, Sunday supplements, weekly and monthly magazines, radio and television programs—sources from which books are reviewed and their authors interviewed and discussed.

Your First Review

If you have a strong literary background, perhaps with one or more degrees in literature or creative writing, you might try your hand at book reviewing. Metropolitan newspapers usually have reviewers and critics on their staffs, but if your local paper publishes book reviews, you might get in touch with its editor. If interested, he or she may want to see samples of your work, and if they are approved, you may be asked to review a book. At this level you will make little if any money at first, but if you polish your skill, in time you can become a skilled reviewer and perhaps some day a full-fledged critic.

Suppose you have decided to initiate your reviewing career with an appraisal of a novel. Before you begin, jot down some reminders to yourself, some steps to guide you toward a successful review.

- Give the book a thorough, thoughtful reading.
- As you read, look for its theme, purpose, and central idea.
- Get a sense of the author's style.
- Note how the book is organized.
- Be aware of both its virtues and its faults.
- Indicate passages suitable for quotation in support of various facets or aspects of the book.
- Keep an open, prejudice-free mind.
- Ask yourself this question: Within the scope of his or her intended purpose as you understand it, has the author failed or succeeded?

Besides fiction (which has shrunk alarmingly in published volume) there are many kinds of nonfiction books to be reviewed, such as histories, biographies, how-to books, children's books, books on economics and politics, travel books, books of poetry, and anthologies. Book reviewing is a craft and a responsibility demanding serious, conscientious work. There are rewards. As a reviewer you will develop new literary insights that may enhance your own writing. In *Coda: Poets and Writers Newsletter,* poet Robert Creeley has said, "I write criticism to clarify my own thinking, not as a defense of my ideas, simply."

Some top publications which print reviews are in the following list. They are well worth studying.

New York Times	*The New Yorker*
Chicago Tribune	*Commonweal*
Christian Science Monitor	*The New Republic*
New York Review of Books	*The Partisan Review*
Harper's Magazine	*The Sewanee Review*

The *Literary Market Place* provides the names and addresses of the book review editors of many newspapers.

DRAMA AND FILM REVIEWS

Big metropolitan newspapers usually have a salaried staff of arts and entertainment writers. Vincent Canby of the *New York Times* is one of these. A first-string critic, Canby generally decides which films will be reviewed. Not all films can be reviewed. In an interview in the spring 1980 *Cineaste,* Canby explains, "The space in the *Times,* is very dear." His kind of criticism is ". . . one man's response to a work, and that response is on several levels—it's analytic, it's expository, descriptive, and personal."

Smaller newspapers often rely on free-lance drama reviewers who cover all important films, the local theater groups, and out-of-town productions. Try viewing a movie or play from a critical point of view, then writing a review of it. Compare your review with that done by a published reviewer. You may be surprised at the originality of your own critical perceptions.

INTERVIEWING

Interviewers, like biographers, ought to have a strong interest in the people they select to interview. The best state in which to approach a subject is a knowledgeable one. If your subject is a person of uncommon interest, read about him or her. Bone up on his or her background and family history. If you are not clear about such details beforehand, you might get yourself tangled in some embarrassing complications, as did the interviewer in the following interview with Leda, of mythological fame.

Interviewer:	*Then your father was Tyndareus?*
Leda:	No, my father was called King Thestius.
Interviewer:	*Ah, yes. King of Troy.*
Leda:	No, no.
Interviewer:	*Ah, I remember now. Thestius was king of Sparta.*
Leda:	I'm afraid not. That was my husband.
Interviewer:	*Thestius?*
Leda:	No. Tyndareus. Thestius was king of Aetolia.
Interviewer:	*I see . . . And you were the mother of Castor and Pollux, the Heavenly Twins?*
Leda:	Yes.
Interviewer:	*Identical twins, weren't they? Hatched from the very same egg?*
Leda:	Not at all! You are very confused.
Interviewer:	*But you laid an egg—*
Leda:	I laid several eggs.
Interviewer:	*But it's in the mythology books that Zeus visited you—ah—disguised as a swan, and you mothered Castor and Pollux?*
Leda:	That much is true. And Zeus *was* the father of Castor. But Pollux hatched from a separate egg, and I have kept his father's name a secret and shall forever.
Interviewer:	*What about Helen? You—uh—laid her, too, didn't you?*

Leda:	Yes, as a matter of fact. And I hatched Clytemnestra, too!
Interviewer:	*And Clytemnestra was the daughter of your mortal husband, Tyndareus?*
Leda:	No, you idiot. I didn't say I *laid* Clytemnestra. I said I *hatched* her. There *is* a difference you know.
Interviewer:	*I give up. Who laid Clytemnestra?*
Leda:	Nemesis. She was a goose—
Interviewer:	*Aha! A goose and a swan . . .*
Leda:	Well, you got *that* part right. Helen's mother was a goose named Nemesis. Her father was a swan. Understand?
Interviewer:	*A certain immortal scoundrel in disguise again?*
Leda:	Yes. Yeats wrote a rather good poem about that situation. In spite of its male chauvinism.
Interviewer:	*Male chauvinism?*
Leda:	Listen, I wasn't all that terrified, and afterwards *he* wasn't all that indifferent, either.

The degree of depth in an interview depends on the nature, purpose, and significance of the interview and the interest your subject's name and personality generates.

As a college student at the University of Minnesota, I carried out several interviews of noted people for a literary magazine of which I was one of the creators, editors, and writers. We called it *The Rejection Slip.* In it we shamelessly printed all our own rejected literary gems and those of our friends, and even an opus or two from faculty members. When George Gershwin came to town to perform, I, the fearless interviewer-in-chief, made an appointment with him. During the interview, by pure intuition and luck, I asked a few of the right questions. Gershwin was charming. He relaxed on a chaise lounge and talked freely about such subjects as his love for Ravel and his preference for beer over champagne. My youthfulness and gross inexperience must have elicited amused tolerance. I was charmed then, but I wince now when I consider what might have been, had I been as adept at the craft of interviewing as I was at arranging the interview. As a music student I was deeply interested in George Gershwin, and he must have felt it, for I was aware that I was not so much handling the interview as I was being given the gift of one by the kindly and generous master musician. This is not an uncommon experience, however, and if you are going to do an interview, do your research, let your interest show, and be prepared to ask a question or two that will lead in the direction you want to go. Your subject will often do the rest, especially if you show genuine interest and honest respect, and do not offend or threaten with crude or over-aggressive interrogation.

Interviews, of course, can be humdrum or heady. If you are deft, it is possible, in a relatively short period of time, to establish an intimate relationship that would be impossible in any other setting.

Ideally such interviews should be held in a quiet atmosphere and at a leisurely pace, though that is not always possible. Also, the interviewer has a choice of taking notes or taping the talk. Taping allows you to observe the expressions and gestures of the interviewee. And he or she must surely find it more interesting to communicate with a responsive face than to view the top of a head bent over a notebook.

Suggested Reading

For good literary interviews, read the *Paris Review,* which has been interviewing noted authors for several decades, *Conversations with Writers* edited by Duggan, Fedricci, and White, and *Contemporary Literary Critics,* published by St. Martin's Press.

Some periodicals containing reviews are *Cineaste, Commentary, Commonweal, Modern Drama, The Nation, New Republic, New Yorker, Partisan Review, Tulane Drama Review, Theatre, Virginia Quarterly Review, American Book Review, The New York Review of Books,* and *Saturday Review.*

CHAPTER 11

FREE-LANCING VIA THE NEWSPAPERS

Every year thousands of free-lance writers submit feature articles to newspapers from coast to coast. The larger Sunday magazines as well as the syndicated publications buy up to ninety-nine percent of their material from free-lancers, according to John P. Hayes, who queried 208 Sunday magazine editors in the United States and Canada. At best this is a part-timer's market, for Sunday supplement articles (excluding the syndicated magazine sections distributed with the Sunday newspaper) ordinarily do not earn large sums of money.

Syndicates sell feature articles to newspapers and get from forty to sixty percent of the proceeds. Rates for syndicated articles vary, depending on the size and circulation of the newspaper or newspapers in which they appear.

Checking the various syndicates listed in *Writer's Market,* you will find that their requirements and needs are quite different. Heritage Features Syndicate, for example (Washington, D.C.), is ninety-nine percent free-lance by writers on contract. It syndicates to over one hundred newspapers, currently needs one-shot features (its newspaper columns are practically all done by regular columnists), and pays $50 minimum.

Fiction Network (San Francisco) is one hundred percent free-lance and syndicates to newspapers and regional magazines. It needs "all types of fiction (particularly holiday) under 2,000 words . . . , specializes in quality literature . . . , pays fifty percent commission . . . , syndicates short fiction only," and encourages previously unpublished authors.

Hispanic Link News Service (Washington, D.C.) needs "magazine columns, magazine features, newspaper columns, newspaper features," preferably "600–700 word op/ed or features, geared to a general national audience," but which "focus on issues or subjects of particular interest to Hispanic Americans . . ." Most of these syndicates will provide writers' guidelines upon request, if a self-addressed, stamped envelope is provided.

Although fifty percent of Sunday magazine articles are written by free-lancers, seventy-five percent of the ideas come from the editors, who then assign articles either to staff members or to free-lancers. To get an idea of the kind of article the various Sunday magazines prefer, read them carefully. Read *Parade, California Living,* or the *Chicago Tribune Sunday Magazine.* Notice the slant. Is it general? Regional? Note the average length of the articles. A very large percent of editors prefer articles from 1,000 to 2,000 words in length, some even less, Hayes's questionnaire revealed.

What do newspapers pay? Generally not much—from $5 to $1,000 or more, depending on circulation. But if you aspire to write full time, the income produced will provide help and encouragement.

CHAPTER 12

PLAYWRIGHTS AND POETS

WRITING PLAYS

Aristotle, as John Howard Lawson said, is "the Bible of playwriting technique." For centuries Aristotle's *Poetics* has been pored over, analyzed, and interpreted, perhaps in as many conflicting ways as the Bible itself. The beginning playwright ought to peruse the playwright's bible, and when viewing or reading a play, note the degree to which Aristotle's ideas on structure, style, and action, conceived over two thousand years ago, are and are not applied today by contemporary playwrights.

Because of religious prejudice against the stage, which was thought to be unedifying and even dissolute, no plays by American playwrights were produced in the colonies until 1766, when *The Prince of Parthia* was staged. None followed until after the American Revolution. Of those written but not produced, some served as pro- and anti-rebel propaganda. Today there is no problem with the morality of the theater—that is, our society no longer discourages all playwriting as an immoral activity—but, of course, this situation can change.

The U.S. Department of Labor's *Dictionary of Occupational Titles* provides the following definition of a playwright:

Writes original plays, such as tragedies, comedies, or dramas, or adapts themes from fictional, historical, or narrative sources, for dramatic presentation: Writes plays, usually involving action, conflict, purpose, and resolution, to depict series of events from imaginary or real life. Writes dialogue and describes action to be followed during enactment of play. Revises script during rehearsals and preparation for initial showing.

The Hurdles

"Very few playwrights I know make their living solely from the theatre ..."

Robert Anderson

For the young playwright the obstacles blocking success are formidable, though not impossible. To begin with, the playwright, like other free-lancers, must, as Robert Anderson says, be a moonlighter. Writing what you believe to be a good play is only the first step. Next there is the business of finding a producer (a feat which even successful playwrights often fail to perform).

If you clear this hurdle, there are before you the many difficulties of play production: the huge expense of theater, director, actors and music. All these problems being resolved, after the first night comes the review. And one bad review from the *New York Times* critic, says Anderson, can "finish off your play."

This is not meant to discourage. There are many opportunities for playwrights today. It is advantageous for the beginner to become involved with a local theater group, meet theater-minded people, and perhaps get his or her play produced. This definitely counts with a publisher. The more you can learn about all the aspects of playwrighting and play production, the better for your future.

Community Production Options

If you think your first play is ready for production, investigate civic theater groups, community theaters, and college and university drama groups in your area. Some of them will be seeking plays to produce. You will not be royally paid, but you will have the exciting pleasure of seeing your characters transformed from words to flesh and of observing the dramatic action you had previously only been able to envision.

Many theaters are seeking new plays. Before submitting a play, however, make sure that the theater is still in the market for material. To give you an idea what types of plays theaters are looking for, here are two examples:

> Woolly Mammoth Theatre Company
> 1317 G St., N.W., Washington, D.C.
> "We look for plays that depart from traditional categories in some way . . . Apart from an innovative approach, there is no formula. One-acts are not used. Cast limit of 8; no unusually expensive gimmicks." Pays 5% royalty.
>
> The Ensemble Studio Theatre
> 549 W. 52nd Street, New York, N.Y. 10019
> "Full lengths and one-acts with strong dramatic actions and situations." Reports in 3 months. Pays $80–$1,000.

Publishers

Play publishers put plays into print and thereby make them available (for a price) to anyone anywhere who may want to produce them. This is done on a royalty basis, with the publisher charging the theater a set rate and usually splitting the sum with the author.

Walter H. Baker Company in Boston, for example, wants

"scripts for amateur production: one-act plays for competition, children's plays, religious drama, monologues, readings, and recitations."

Samuel French (New York) wants "full-length plays for dinner, community, stock, college, high school, and church theatres. One-act plays (30 to 60 minutes) for high school and college theatres. Children's plays, 45 to 75 minutes. Payment is on a royalty basis."

SCRIPTS FOR THE SCREENS

A screen writer is a scriptwriter who wants to break into motion pictures. According to the *Dictionary of Occupational Titles,* here's what he or she does:

> Writes scripts for motion pictures or television: Selects subject and theme for script based on personal interest or assignment. Conducts research to obtain accurate factual background information and authentic detail. Writes plot outline, narrative synopsis, or treatment and submits for approval. Confers with PRODUCER (motion pic.) or PRODUCER (radio & tv broad.) and DIRECTOR, MOTION PICTURE (motion pic.) or DIRECTOR, TELEVISION (radio & tv broad.) regarding script development, revisions, and other changes. Writes one or more drafts of script. May work in collaboration with other writers. May adapt books or plays into scripts for use in television or motion picture production. May write continuity or comedy routines. May specialize in particular type of script or writing.

Writing for the Small Screen

Although the free-lance television market is difficult to crack, there are ways to break in and snare lucrative assignments, says Andy Edmonds. She ought to know. She is a writer/producer who has worked on both network and cable television and whose credits include "Family Ties" and "All in the Family." In her November 1987 *Writer's Digest* article "Breaking Into TV Scriptwriting," Edmonds suggests rules that will "point you in the right direction." In summary, here they are:

- Write a sample script—an episode of a TV series (an established and not a new one) currently in production.
- Get an agent.
- Be aggressively persistent.
- Be prepared to meet with producers and "pitch" story ideas, and to elaborate fully on any ideas you present.

Edmonds elaborates on each point—how to choose the right series for your sample, how to approach the writing of your script, how to get the best agent as a new writer, and what you can earn. In the second part of this article Bob Ellison writes, "It is among the most coveted of all writing assignments—the go-ahead to create an episode for a network television series. It's one of the most profitable, too—$17,134 minimum." Bob Ellison's scripts have been sold to "The Insiders" and "Hart to Hart."

What about Hollywood?

A few years ago Ben Stein wrote a somewhat sobering book about Hollywood writers. In it, he reveals some interesting facts. The writers of network shows number only a few hundred. One, Stephen Kandel, who was interviewed by Stein, has written pilots and scripts for "Wonder Woman," "Star Trek," "Cannon," "Hawaii Five-O," "The Bionic Woman," "The Six Million Dollar Man," "Barnaby Jones," "Streets of San Francisco," "Switch," "Mannix," and "Mission Impossible." According to Stein, all of the regular working writers have a "unified, idiosyncratic view of life, and almost all of them live in Los Angeles." Their views, Stein writes, "could not possibly be the dreams of a nation." TV, then, mirrors what these few people think.

It was estimated that only eight out of twenty good scripts got to be pilots, and only two became series. Of these, the most durable, according to Stein, were situation comedies and adventure shows. Scripts then and now are almost never the work of one person, and the writer has very little control over the finished product. In *Reel People* by Mark Litwak, one apparently successful screenwriter commented:

> "They ruin your stories. They massacre your ideas. They prostitute your art. They trample your pride. And what do you get for it? A fortune."

YOUR EDUCATION

If you are intent upon free-lancing in the film and broadcast media and want to become more knowledgeable or wish to update your educational background and qualifications, colleges and universities can help you. Courses are available in scriptwriting (introduction to the fundamentals of film, radio, and TV scriptwriting); in broadcast writing (lecture and laboratory courses in writing for broadcasting); and in creative writing for film (intensive workshops in the advanced stages of motion picture scriptwriting). There may also be an adult school or community college in your area offering relevant courses.

THE DRAMATISTS GUILD

Anyone who has authored one full-length play may apply for membership in the Dramatists Guild. Applications are voted on. The guild exists "to protect and promote the professional interests of authors of dramatic and dramatic-musical works, to protect rights in such works, and to improve the conditions under which their works are created and produced." It also formulates types of production contracts with respect to dramatic and dramatic-musical works. When a writer joins the Dramatists Guild, he or she automatically becomes a member of the Authors League of America.

Suggested Reading

Drama A to Z lists alphabetically five hundred commonly used words and phrases, from *ab ovo* to *zarzuela* (a form of Spanish lyric theater). It also includes "A Chronology of Dramatic Theory and Criticism," in which each entry is considered a milestone in the writing of dramatic criticism. *The American Film Industry* by Tino Balio presents a comprehensive view of the industry. It was published by the University of Wisconsin Press in 1986. You will find books on screenwriting, editing, and playwrighting in most bookstores and public libraries.

POETRY

> "Who are professors that they should attempt to deal
> with a thing as fine and high as poetry?"
>
> —Robert Frost

A poet is a miner-magician who can retrieve gold nuggets from mined-out rivers and polish them to an insightful sparkle. Some poets mine their own dark souls and stun or spangle the imagination with their findings. Poets have the gift of a mysterious fifth force by which they strip big and little things—a humiliated planet or a proud little rock—down to an incredible essence.

And poetry isn't profitable—that's the bottom line. Should you find acceptance in one of the forty to fifty poetry magazines, expect nothing more than $50 and a free copy, or nothing at all. In some cases you must even pay for your copy.

Your reward will be visibility and the joy of being published, which translates into being heard, perhaps even quoted.

Some literary and little magazines accept poetry. The *Hudson Review* pays 50¢ a line; the *Denver Quarterly,* $20 a printed page; the *Partisan Review,* $25 a poem; and *Plowshares,* $10 per poem. Recognized poets, no doubt, do much better.

I have given you the financial facts, knowing that you would not be working with a difficult genre like poetry if you were not vitally aware of the highest reward of all, when words in patterns transcend their solitary meanings and a thought takes on form, life, and spirit, and you have created something lovely and lasting, something "high and fine."

For information on current market needs, writers' and poets' conferences and colonies, fairs and festivals, grants and awards, and professional or how-to advice, read *Coda: Poets and Writers Newsletter,* published four times a year.

Suggested Reading

Adcock, Fleur, ed. *Twentieth Century Women's Poetry.* London, 1987.

Breed, Paul I., and Florence M. Sniderman. *Dramatic Criticism Index: A Bibliography on Playwrights from Ibsen to Avant-Garde.* Detroit: Gale Research Company, 1972.

Deutch, Babette. *Poetry Handbook: A Dictionary of Terms.* New York: Funk and Wagnall's.

Ellman, Richard, and Robert O'Clair, eds. *The Norton Anthology of Modern Poetry.* New York, 1973.

Hamilton, Anne. *Seven Principles of Poetry.* Boston: The Writer, Inc.

McGraw-Hill Encyclopedia of World Drama. 4 vols. New York: McGraw-Hill Book Company, 1972.

Paz, Octavio, comp. *Mexican Poetry: An Anthology.* Translated by Samuel Becket. New York, 1985.

Smiley, Sam. *Playwrighting: The Structure of an Action.* Englewood Cliffs: Prentice-Hall, 1971.

Van Druten, John. *Playwright at Work.* New York: Harper and Brothers, 1953.

Wagner, Jean. *Black Poets of the United States.* Urbana: University of Illinois Press, 1973.

Roger Ebert, nationally recognized movie critic, began his career as a
newspaper reporter. (photo courtesy of Roger Ebert)

CHAPTER 13

JOURNALISM YESTERDAY, TODAY, AND TOMORROW

Major journalism in America up until the twentieth century was, by and large, political and partisan. Most of the early colonial newspapers before 1765 were published in seaports. There was little popular culture or education. These were pioneer times, and the principal concern was to survive and build for the future in a frontier environment. For the always news-hungry population there were the professional newsletters that came from England on sailing ships. Local writers composed pamphlets, and rhymesters wrote ballads about local scandal and hawked them on the streets.

The first issue of the first colonial paper appeared in 1690. It was called *Publick Occurrences Both Foreign and Domestick.* Alas, its first issue was its last issue; the governor and council suppressed it, most likely because, in addition to local news, it carried some military information that was not intended for the public.

The enactment of the Stamp Act in 1765 stirred patriot papers to violent opposition. During the American Revolution it became the duty of patriotic people to collect rags to be made into paper. After the war, newspaper publishing spread gradually across the new country, usually allying with particular political groups or movements. In the late nineteenth century, newspapers began detaching themselves from political party commitment or control to become independent. By 1950, half the daily papers in the United States described themselves as independent.

THE PRESS, THE REPORTER, AND THE PUBLIC

In our complex world, relationships between the press, the public, and world events are complicated and go far beyond the traditional ingredients of a news story: the who, what, when, where, why, and how. Questions a reporter does and does not ask, and answers and explanations he or she includes or excludes, may possibly influence the future course of events and alter the lives of the people they affect. The reporter's job demands a sense of responsibility and respect for the truth. The ability to write accurately and with clarity under pressure, the exercise of tact, objective judgment, and responsibility, must be brought to the writing of a news story.

Journalism as a career is newspapers, television, radio, advertising, promotion, public relations, teaching journalism, magazines, wire services, and photojournalism—a wide choice which necessitates attending a school of journalism for today's young journalist.

Journalism is an exciting but highly competitive occupation. Make sure you have sufficient motivation and capabilities before enrolling in a school. Are you really interested enough to work toward such a challenging career? Are your high school and college grades above average? Are you proficient in reading, writing, spelling, and grammar? Journalism schools are raising their standards. Upon graduation don't expect to go right to work for a big city newspaper. Get experience with smaller papers first.

The Reporter's Job

Suppose you definitely intend to become a news reporter. Some of the options are listed below:

newspaper reporter
news magazine reporter
radio news reporter
television news reporter
news agency reporter

The newspaper reporter performs the following tasks:

1. He or she collects news, talks to observers, gets accurate information about what has happened, where, when, to whom, how, and why.
2. The reporter calls in to the city editor of the paper and reports what he or she has learned.
3. Then, either the reporter returns to the newsroom and writes the story, or, if he or she must cover another story, the first story is given by telephone to a rewrite person.
4. And then? Perhaps the reporter must cover a controversial conservation commission meeting, or be at the airport with questions when a visiting dignitary arrives, or he or she might be asked to report on a speech to be made by the mayor at a senior citizen's center.

SPECIAL FIELDS OF REPORTING

The *investigative reporter* writes stories that involve days or perhaps weeks of reporting about problems facing the community and the nation.

Specialty reporters have "beats" such as courts, business, medicine, politics, city government, and foreign affairs. After months or years of experience, a general assignment reporter might advance to one of these two positions.

Newspapers hire *writers*—experienced and talented writers—to write editorials and columns. These writers generally present their own or their newspaper's opinion or position in their comments.

All reporters are writers, of course, and whatever the type of work, there will be challenge, excitement, and the pressure of deadlines to meet, sometimes long and irregular hours, and even, on occasion, danger.

YESTERDAY'S NEWS REPORTER

Yesterday's newsman, as portrayed in Hecht and MacArthur's play, *Front Page* (the movie was entitled *Front Page Story*) was street-wise, tough, unscrupulous, and sometimes given to torturing the truth for the sake of a sensational story. A heavy-drinking, smart-talking cynic living from hand to mouth, he was unconscionably exploited by his editor. The character Hildy Johnson, a Chicago reporter, is described as a "vanishing type—the lusty, hoodlumesque, half-drunken caballero . . ." whom journalism schools and the advertising business "have nearly extirpated."

Those words were written in 1930. Hildy Johnson represented the stage and cinema stereotype of that period in newspaper history.

TODAY'S NEWS REPORTER

Ideally, today's journalist is serious-minded, has a sense of public responsibility, and strives to report the news objectively, factually, and fairly. He or she comes to journalism with a college degree, perhaps in journalism. The reporter's educational and cultural background will have prepared her or him to approach events, personalities, and institutions in the community, city, and country with understanding and intelligence.

WHERE JOURNALISM GRADS GO TO WORK

Here are some figures on the 21,100 graduates of the class of 1986, taken from a survey conducted by the Dow Jones Newspaper Fund.

Jobs with media-related companies declined almost 4 percent from 1985, while jobs found with other employers increased by 2.5 percent. The breakdown:

media employers	51.4%
promoting a company or product	28.6%
graduate school	7.5%
unemployed	12.5%

The following categories describe the types of jobs taken by graduates involved in media-related work:

writing and/or editing	35.8%
promoting a company or product	12.5%
designing and/or selling advertising	6.7%
production	3.5%
photography, graphics, art, or cartooning	2.4%

Daily and weekly newspapers and news services hired 3,270 journalism and mass communications graduates in 1986. Radio and television stations hired approximately 1,752 of these graduates. Advertising agencies and public relations departments hired 1,836 journalism grads in 1986. Median annual starting salaries are estimated as follows:

public relations	$15,300
advertising agencies	14,700
daily newspapers	13,900
radio and television stations	12,600

ELECTRONIC JOURNALISM

There have been many new technological developments in broadcast journalism, and more are in progress. Electronic journalists work with microphones and tapes and audio and audio-visual equipment and devices to help achieve instantaneous transcription, sometimes reporting the news live by radio or television as it happens. The TV news reporter has a triple responsibility: to get the facts, the sound, and the moving picture with the assistance of a camera and sound crew. TV news comes from a variety of reporters. There are foreign correspondents, local or regional field reporters, political reporters, environmental reporters, and sports reporters. Besides his or her other duties, even the anchorperson, highest paid of all, may have a hand in writing the newscasting program.

The future will hold more technological advances and demand more education and more special training.

Other Writing-related Newspaper Jobs

THE COPY EDITOR

According to the *Newspaper Fund Guide,* at most newspapers the *copy editor* job is considered an entry-level position involving "great attention to detail, accuracy and possible libel, as well as an advanced command of the language." It also points out that "newspaper careers as editors can start at that level, and the copy editor may advance directly to higher editing positions without years of reporting experience." A newspaper copy editor may be promoted to the position of departmental editor or may become an editorial writer, a columnist, or a critic.

THE MANAGING EDITOR

The top newsroom employee is the *managing editor,* who earns an average salary of $44,177 annually, according to an Inland Daily Press Association wage and salary survey. By mid-1987, on the other hand, the average for all reporters in the survey was only $15,387.

There are multiple reasons 1986 graduates preferred radio or advertising to print jobs, beginning possibly with the low pay and scarcity of jobs in the print sector, where the standards in writing skills are more demanding. Perhaps another reason is broadcasting and advertising promise more glamour. Whatever the reasons, the number of news-ed majors has declined nationwide, and only sixty-four percent of the 1986 graduates who joined the work force got newspaper jobs—at an average salary of $13,900.

THE MOST VALUABLE BACKGROUND FOR A JOURNALISM CAREER

If you have determined that journalism is for you, a two-year study by the Journalism Educational Association released in 1986 found that "an academic-based journalism program is one of the most valuable high school curriculum offerings to teach students communications skills and freedom of expression concepts." It was found that students who "have worked on high school newspapers and yearbooks score significantly higher on various ACT tests than do those students who have not had such high school experiences."

THE 1987 JOURNALISM CAREER AND SCHOLARSHIP GUIDE

Prepared by the Dow Jones Newspaper Fund, Inc., this extensive guide is an indispensable tool for anyone considering a career in any segment of the newsprint industry. It provides an overview of news careers, describes how to apply for a newspaper job, lists universities that offer journalism majors, and includes a directory of journalism scholarships.

Copies are generally available through journalism departments, career counseling and guidance centers, and public and college libraries. If necessary, you can write for a copy to The Dow Jones Newspaper Fund, Post Office Box 300, Princeton, N.J. 08543-0300.

ROGER EBERT: DISTINGUISHED NEWSPAPER REPORTER, AUTHOR, AND FILM CRITIC

Roger Ebert, nationally recognized and admired by TV viewers, began his career in journalism at Urbana, Illinois, when he "purchased a Hektograph set . . . that allowed me to hand-letter a neighborhood newspaper and then use a tray of gelatin to reproduce several smudged, purple copies of the *Washington Street News.*" He produced his own publications during grade school and high school, and got a job as a part-time sportswriter at age fifteen; even before he graduated from high school he "graduated" to "the state and city desks of the *News-Gazette* in Urbana, writing obituaries and covering traffic accidents, county fairs, and Rotary Club meetings."

At the University of Illinois, Ebert said, he got invaluable experience working on the *Daily Illini,* "one of the nation's great college papers."

Ebert claims that he became a movie critic "through good luck. I was always a movie fan." At screenings of campus film societies at the University of Illinois, Ebert said, he saw great classics such as "*The Four Hundred Blows, Oharu, Hiroshima mon Amour, The Maltese Falcon,* and *Swing Time.*"

In 1966, he joined the *Chicago Sun-Times* as a general assignment feature writer; then, with no experience, he was appointed film critic, replacing a retired predecessor. "I learned on the job," he explained, "as many journalists have done on many beats for many years . . . I learned that it was possible to express a personal style while still observing the discipline of newspaper style."

Ebert considers job prospects for aspiring movie critics to be "not good." Employment opportunities in the field, according to Ebert, are very limited. "My advice? First, become a good, competent reporter . . . Then get a wide background in the arts, so that you'll be qualified for an employer who might want you to review plays and dance and gallery openings as well as movies or television."

"I think of myself primarily as a newspaperman. I never really aimed for a career in television, did not audition for the program I do with Gene Siskel, and am still somewhat amazed to find myself on the tube every week. I will say that I think our show benefits mightily from the backgrounds in daily journalism that we both bring to it."

Roger Ebert's advice to anyone aspiring to a newspaper career: "Start at the earliest possible age to write for whatever publication will print your work . . . Aim to work for a local publication where you can actually see your work in print fairly quickly, and where you can work beside more experienced journalists. Don't worry about the pay, the experience is worth much more."

REPORTING FOR THE OTHER MEDIA

News Magazine Reporting

Here the key word is not writing, but research. The news magazine reporter gathers data. A staff writer will write the story. The magazine news reporter's researching entails gathering facts and data directly from people who are involved in the story and written or printed material in files, records, and books, wherever they may be. Interviewing, if not feasible by telephone, may necessitate traveling, sometimes long distances.

Unlike that of the newspaper reporter's, the life of a news magazine reporter is not a hectic one. But he or she must be an experienced, skilled researcher to do this job well.

Eric Taub, West Coast bureau chief for the weekly publication *Cablevision* is "a reporter, critic, and analyst" who digs, deciphers, and stays on top of the industry and the state of the art, which can change every day. "A good reporter has to be concise. You have to be a tight writer. You also have to read a lot about the industry . . . Surprisingly, there are still a lot of solid opportunities for people who know how to write and who know about cable," Taub said.

WRITING FOR THE WIRE SERVICES

The wire services also employ reporters, rewrite men and women, and editors. The Associated Press is the world's oldest and largest news-gathering cooperative (owned by its American newspaper and broadcast members). Barry Hanson of the corporate communications department kindly provided the following information.

"Using satellite and land communications, the Associated Press's staff of 2,850 people disseminates news and pictures to more than 1,400 daily newspapers and 6,400 radio and television stations in the United States and to 8,500 foreign subscribers in 115 countries. In the United States, 1,100 employees work in the production of news and photos in 142 news bureaus and the New York headquarters. The news cooperative has bureaus in all 50 states."

"The AP foreign staff is made up of 480 news and photo staffers in 84 bureaus in 70 countries."

Regarding wages, Mr. Hanson stated, "Current weekly wage scales for the domestic news and photo staff range from

$386.85 per week to start up to a minimum of $653 after five years. Wage scales are similar for the foreign service."

Generally AP's requirements for employment in the news and photo staff include a college education and a minimum of two years' professional experience on a daily newspaper or in a news department of a radio or television station. For those who hope someday to work for the wire services, the best training experience would be to work as a general assignment reporter on a small or medium-sized newspaper for two years or so, concentrating on accuracy, speed, and all-around news abilities.

BEFORE YOU MATRICULATE

How genuine is your interest in journalism? Make sure before you enroll in a school of journalism that you have the qualifications and the motivation sufficient to pursue such a career. Try furnishing some thoughtful answers to these questions.

Am I strong on curiosity about people and events?

Do I have a pleasant, outgoing personality?

Can I maintain poise and confidence, keep my head, and get the facts straight in taxing, confusing situations?

Is persistence one of my traits?

Am I, or can I learn to be, a diligent researcher?

Will I enjoy writing on a daily basis?

Can I maintain one hundred percent accuracy?

Can I work well under pressure?

Will I be satisfied to work irregular and sometimes long hours?

Will I be satisfied to work from the bottom up?

If you can answer "yes" to these questions, you have some of the basic qualifications of a news reporter.

Suggested Reading

The Columbia Journalism Review.

Facts about Newspapers. A statistical summary of the newspaper business published by the American Newspaper Publishers' Association.

The Journalism Career and Scholarship Guide. 1987. Published by the Newspaper Fund.

Read All about It: A Day in the Life of a Metropolitan Newspaper. Jane T. Harragan, 1987.

CHAPTER 14

WRITERS IN BROADCASTING

THE TELEVISION PICTURE

The invention of television might be attributed to a long, long list of scientists and technologists from many countries, beginning in 1839 with Alexandre Edmond Becquerel, who discovered the electro-chemical effects of light, which culminated in V. K. Zworykin's ionoscope camera tube, patented in 1923, and the invention of the cathode-ray tube in 1932.

The regular broadcasting of television—the electrical transmission of pictures in motion and the simultaneous electrical transmission of the accompanying sounds—began on a regular basis in 1941. Its impact on social, political, and cultural life in the United States has been immense.

Think of it. Television, for better or for worse, has become the principal means by which Americans maintain contact with the daily flow of national life. It has entered our homes and our minds and rearranged our lives and our thoughts. Next to parents, it is probably the most potent cultural influence on our children. It is our chief form of entertainment, and it is beginning to preempt the newspaper as our primary source of news. By means of its worldwide coverage of major world events (for example, the Vietnam War and the struggle for power in the Middle East and Africa), it has reduced our concept of the dimensions of our planet. With its coverage of the space exploration of astronauts and unmanned satellites it has taken us to the outskirts of our solar system. After Pluto—what? Like Galileo and the telescope it has diminished our sense of our significance in the universal order of things and filled us with awe at the immensity and grandeur of the cosmos.

Boon or Bane?

David Sarnoff, chairman of the Radio Corporation of America at the time of the dedication ceremonies of the RCA Exhibit building at the 1939 World's Fair, said of the new medium, "It is a creative force which we must learn to utilize for the benefit of all mankind."

Critic John J. O'Connor of the *New York Times* has remarked recently in one of his columns that television is "at least 90% trash." Most everyone has heard it labelled "a wasteland."

Today the "electronic Cyclops," as Hal Himmelstein calls it in *On the Small Screen,* is an ever-present, pervasive force exercising both positive and negative influences on our everyday lives. Its influence on the lives of young people is amazing: some consider it dangerous and destructive of humanistic values.

The flaws and weaknesses of TV are of a disturbing magnitude. Its programs, its news, the material in its editorials, and its advertisers' commercials comprise, collectively, a complex collage of audio-visual suggestions, an insistent image allegedly expressing the reality of American life. Its messages and values daily reinforce this image of our society. Since most of its programming is paid for by advertisers, the name of the game becomes ratings, the highest profit coming from those programs gaining the largest number of consumers/listeners.

Who controls the quantity and quality of network broadcasting, roughly two-thirds of what we see? Since there are many advertisers and only three networks, the networks (under the advertising time restrictions imposed by the Federal Communications Commission) control quantity. As for quality, it is said that the public—by what it buys and what it doesn't buy in the marketplace—makes the ultimate choice. But generally speaking, the choice offered the public is limited and uninspiring—trivia, banality, stereotypes, violence, excessive sex, aggrandizement of wealth and the acquisitive drive, and political slanting by exclusion. With notable and memorable exceptions, this is at least a portion of the dreary side of the commercial television picture as we see it now. But television, through its news coverage, its documentaries, its interviews, and its cultural and science programs, has also taken us to corners of the world we could hardly imagine and brought us essential knowledge and inspiring views of great artists.

In this controversial, chaotic, and exciting medium, what are the opportunities for writers?

WRITING OPPORTUNITIES IN TV AND RADIO

The News Reporter

The TV and radio reporters' jobs parallel the newspaper news reporters', but in conformity with the prescribed editorial style and format standards of their particular media. One radical difference is that both must be prepared to conduct live interviews or describe pertinent details from the site of an event or mobile broadcast; but of course the television reporter, with the help of a sound and camera crew, is seen as well as heard.

TV and radio news reporters may also transmit data to a newswriter, who will then write the story. And like the newspaper news reporter, they may specialize in one type of reporting, such as sports, political affairs, court trials, or police activities.

Assigned to outlying areas or to a foreign country, the TV news reporter will be designated *correspondent* or *foreign correspondent.* As a specialist, he or she may be a consumer affairs reporter, an urban reporter, or a business reporter. Like other news reporting jobs, the work varies from dull and tedious to exciting and dangerous.

The Newswriter

TV and radio newswriters write stories for publication or broadcast from the written or recorded notes they receive from the reporting staff. Reviewing and evaluating this material, they must verify its accuracy and check questionable facts and details. The writer may also be required to consult files and other reference sources for supplemental information to add to the story. Then he or she must rewrite it in conformity with a specified length and style. When the occasion demands, the writer also must be capable of writing under pressure. As members of the Writers Guild of America, newswriters at top-market local stations can earn between $35,000 and $45,000 per year, and top newswriters in the big markets are said to earn over $50,000.

The Continuity Writer

The continuity writer, working under a continuity director, originates and prepares material which the announcer reads. This writer's function is to introduce and connect the various parts of musical, news, and sports programs.

The Editorial Writer

Editorialism has become prevalent in TV broadcasting. The editorialist, by researching and taking a stand on local affairs, brings the station and the community closer together. A firm position on local or state social, economic, or cultural problems may elicit strong pro and con responses from listeners. For this reason the editorialist must base the editorial posture on sound research and accurate data if he or she is to make practical recommendations for change.

The editorial writer may specialize in such fields as international affairs, fiscal matters, or local or national politics.

The Commentator

Like the editorialist, the commentator may record or present the commentary live. He or she is responsible for gathering information and developing a subject perspective through interviews, experience, and sometimes by attendance at functions such as political conventions, news meetings, sports events, and social activities. The commentator formulates his or her analysis and interpretation into a story idea, organizes it into acceptable medium form and style, and writes the commentary. If the commentator analyzes current news items, he or she may be designated *news analyst.*

The Newscaster

Regular daily appearances on TV news programs make the newscaster a familiar and often a very popular personality.

Since his or her personality is instrumental in building a wide audience, he or she must be an attractive, personable individual with a pleasing voice who can communicate with clarity and authority. Network newscasters like Tom Brokaw and Dan Rather tend to be formal, whereas local newscasters are more personal and chatty, and they often ad lib.

Newscasters either determine the selection of news items to be broadcast or are assigned them by an editorial staff. The newscaster may prepare or assist in preparation of the TV or radio script.

The News Director

Would you like to become a news director? This is the top job in news. The news director is in charge of the TV or radio news operation. It is the news director who sets policies and makes decisions on news coverage and presentation, hires and assigns members of the staff, and is the administrative link between the news operation and the station management. Most news directors have been reporters, assignment editors, and/or producers before being promoted. The best educational background is a liberal arts education stressing language skills, history, government, and the social sciences, with journalism as either a major or minor. Depending on the size of the newsroom, the news director usually spends very little time writing and most in administrative duties.

HOW TO QUALIFY FOR A CAREER IN BROADCASTING

If you are aiming for a career in broadcasting, the Radio-Television News Directors Association offers the following suggestions for getting started on your way:

- Learn grammar, composition, and clear expression.
- Get experience in public speaking or debate.
- Learn to type.
- Do beginning work in news and broadcasting—a school paper, free-lance work in news, or announcing or production at a local radio or TV station on or off campus.
- Become well-read and well-informed in a wide variety of areas.
- Visit radio or TV stations in your area. (Make an appointment.)
- Make sure three-fourths of your education is in liberal arts.

WHAT YOU CAN EARN IN RADIO AND TV NEWS BROADCASTING

Of the four categories of mass communications—daily newspapers, radio/TV stations, advertising agencies, and public relations, median starting salaries in radio/TV in 1986 were lowest, according to the Dow Jones 1987 *Career and Scholarship Guide.*

After forty years of robust growth, significant changes have occurred in the TV industry during the last two years. The three networks, CBS, ABC, and NBC, are now in the hands of new owners, and the broadcasting industry has experienced a period of retrenchment. The new owners want to make more profits through decreasing costs. According to *Channels* magazine, the results are salary decreases in the middle and lower ranks, "while top executives continue to reward themselves with generous salary hikes and bonuses." Consequently, the average compensation for two top executives rose 11.7 percent last year, while TV news salaries climbed by just 2.2 percent, according to a survey conducted by the Radio-Television News Directors Association. Figures from the

Federal Bureau of Labor Statistics tell the same story. For example, salaries of nonsupervisory and production employees in all broadcasting declined from $10.96 an hour in January 1986 to $10.75 an hour in January 1987.

Channels also reported that salary increases within television news departments "trailed behind both national trends and the hefty gains of earlier years," and the RTNDA stated that "median salaries for rank and file TV anchors and reporters remained virtually the same, at $26,000 and $16,900 respectively, although in radio broadcasting there was a rise of 16 percent in median pay."

OPPORTUNITIES IN CABLE

"Cable may be television's growth industry," according to Joseph Vitale in *Channels* magazine (July/August 1987), "but you'd never know it by salaries at the system level." "Impact '86," a study that details cable's impact on the economy, has shown that while cable contributed 25 billion dollars to the GNP in 1986 and has experienced explosive growth during the 1980s, the wage gap between cable and broadcast TV is wide, and although cable has created thousands of new jobs, over ninety percent of its employees are working at the systems level.

Cable programmers' total cost for products purchased from motion picture studios and other members of the production community neared one billion dollars in 1986 (with theatrical products from premium programmers accounting for sixty percent), so obviously there are opportunities for free-lance scriptwriters in cable as well as in broadcast TV. Though writers come first, they are the last to share in the profits. Production companies create TV mini-series and movies. It takes close to one hundred people to produce a half-hour situation comedy. But there are positive rewards;

for example, successful scriptwriter Melanie Mintz earned $16,144 per episode of "Knots Landing."

But *The Writer* provides a *nota bene*: the TV market is a difficult one to break into. "All submissions must be made through registered agents as, in general, direct submissions of scripts, no matter how good they are, are not considered by producers and programmers." Writers should concentrate on getting their fiction (short or in novel form) and nonfiction published in magazines or books, which are combed by television producers for possible adaptations. Adaptations from what has appeared in print constitute a large percentage of the material shown on all types of networks.

The *cable newswriter* writes what the anchor reads. The copy must keep pace with the news as it happens, and is obtained from the wire services and other sources. It must be transmitted rapidly from newswriter to producer to newsreader or anchor. The cable newswriter's annual salary is estimated to be between $12,000 and $20,000. Newswriters' salaries are higher in broadcast TV. Network newswriters average $42,328, and in large markets top writers may earn over $50,000.

For those who want a career in cable TV, there's plenty to learn. Universities with broadcasting departments are including cable in their programs, and some cable companies have established interning programs for students of the industry.

Suggested Reading

Van Nostren, William. *The Nonbroadcast Television Writer's Handbook.*
Bagdikian, Ben H. *The Media Monopoly.*
Brown, Les. *Television: The Business Behind the Box.*
Burnett, Hallie. *The Screenwriter's Handbook.*

Maloney, Martin. *Writing for the Media.*
National Association of Broadcasters. *Careers in Radio.*
Balio, Tina. *The American Film Industry.*
Ellis, Elmo. *Opportunities in Broadcasting Careers.*
Bone, Jan. *Opportunities in Cable Television Careers.*
Noronha, Shonan. *Opportunities in Television and Video Careers.*

CHAPTER 15

WRITERS IN ADVERTISING

Advertising, like broadcasting with which it is closely allied, is regarded by many people as a glamorous industry. Others consider it a sort of parasitic monster that preys on people by inducing them (often subliminally) to buy products they don't need and, in the process, adding to the cost of those products. In any case, advertising is a key force in our economy which uses every available medium to sell products, services, and institutions to the American consumer.

Advertising has been around a long time. Its first medium was the human voice. Sale of slaves, livestock, and so forth was advertised by criers in ancient times. The coming of movable type around 1450 brought the inception of mass media advertising in its wake, but only after the appearance of the newspaper. In 1666, the *London Gazette* announced that advertising the sale of books, medicines, and other things was "not properly the business of a Paper of Intelligence," and that "a Paper of Advertisements will be forthwith printed apart, and recommended to the Publick by another hand." Thus was born the first advertising supplement.

With the rise and burgeoning of industrialism the advertising business expanded proportionately. The growth of the magazine market and mass transportation created larger and larger audiences. By the end of the nineteenth century, hundreds of millions of dollars were being spent by advertisers. By 1966, advertising expenditures had risen to $16,500,000,000.

Almost every kind of business or industry uses advertising to create a demand for its products and services. American advertisers believe the consumer needs to be informed of new and available goods and services, and the American Advertising Federation claims that advertising is simply the cheapest way to provide that information.

Advertising is vitally important in the communications industry, for the profits of many of the media depend principally upon the dollars advertisers spend. Agencies range in size from one person to thousands of people. Some are specialized, and some are what are called full service advertising agencies.

A lot of interesting and talented people have worked in advertising. Among them, working at the copywriter's job, were Hart Crane, Sinclair Lewis, Theodore Dreiser, Sherwood Anderson, Cornelia Otis Skinner, Dorothy Parker—and even Bob Newhart.

Besides the agencies, where do people get jobs in advertising? In the ad departments of manufacturing firms, retail stores, banks, power companies, professional and trade associations, and many other organizations at local, regional, and national levels. Printers, art studios, letter shops, package design firms, and similar businesses often employ advertising people. Small business owners are experiencing a growing need for professional advertising. However, the job competition is keen because "the glamorous nature of the field" attracts many people, says the U.S. Labor Department's *Occupational Outlook Handbook.*

What sort of work does advertising have to offer the writer?

THE ADVERTISING COPYWRITER

A job at the very heart of the industry, composing the advertising message, is the job of the *copywriter.* Copy is the verbal portion of an ad, the printed words in a magazine, newspaper, or direct mail ad, or the spoken words in a TV or radio commercial. It is the copywriter's job to motivate large masses of people. The message must influence them to accept an idea or to purchase a product or service, or have faith or confidence in a business or other institution.

The copywriter studies the product and its potential market, special groups of customers such as teenagers, sports lovers, business executives, or homemakers. He or she conceives and develops the text to be used in the ad.

A copywriter may work under an account executive or a copy chief or copy supervisor, who in turn reports to a creative director. He or she may be teamed with an art director and a TV producer. Applying the English language to stimulate product/service/idea acceptance and sales is the job and the responsibility of a good copywriter.

Copywriters also write publicity releases, promotional or informational booklets, sales-promotion materials, merchandising campaigns, radio and TV commercials, trade journal articles about products and services, and rewrites of existing copy.

Supplementary to their writing, copywriters may be expected to research information or confer with advertisers, and that of course calls for clear, concise, and enthusiastic articulation of an idea or plan. As in most advertising jobs, a college education is essential to the copywriter. Added to that, some practical experience in writing, perhaps for a college or community newspaper, is helpful in developing writing skills.

What do you take with you as you seek your first job in advertising?

1. A résumé, including all previous employment and extracurricular and community activities, especially those involving writing, promotion, sales, or research; any special award or commendations you have received; an outline of your educational background along with degrees and honors attained; and a list of references from people familiar with your character and capabilities.
2. A portfolio containing samples of your work, such as editorials, promotional letters, and news columns. The material should be carefully and interestingly arranged.
3. A cheerful attitude, a list of questions concerning the company and the nature and responsibilities of the job, and the desire to represent your assets and abilities with frankness and clarity.

An aspiring advertising copywriter ought to be well aware of the effects of advertising on viewers and readers. Many knowledgeable people believe that advertising can change behavior and alter people's lives. And the determination of how and in what direction is a responsibility which the copywriter must share.

What Do Copywriters Earn?

Salaries vary, depending on the region. In 1986, the median annual salary in advertising agencies was $32,500, according to *Adweek* magazine, and the salary range was from $30,000 to $60,000.

Data from the American Advertising Federation show that in general, beginning salaries vary, but most junior copywriters start out between $10,000 to $15,000. Senior positions are more competitive, and their salaries range from $20,000 upward.

A FRAMEWORK FOR ADVERTISING ETHICS

An "Advertising Code of American Business," published by the American Advertising Federation as a framework for advertising ethics, states, among other things, that advertising "shall tell the truth" and "provide substantiation of claims made; avoid violations of good taste and public decency, false or misleading statements, and disparagements of competitors' products and services; and avoid false, misleading, exaggerated or unprovable claims."

Does advertising stay within these guidelines? Not all advertisers do, certainly, and some criticism comes from within the industry itself. A case in point is the current controversy over ads demeaning and humiliating to women. As the co-owner of a small San Francisco agency said recently, "Certainly women are exploited by advertising. But so are men." He added, "It's a bad ad if it doesn't sell," a philosophy which seems to clash head-on with the American Advertising Federation's code.

SCHOOLS WITH PROGRAMS IN ADVERTISING

Advertising Education Publications, 3429 55th Street, Lubbock, Texas 79413, has published a pamphlet entitled "Where Shall I Go to School to Study Advertising?" Schools listed are designed to "educate students interested in a career in advertising." Programs are either in journalism, with an emphasis on the creative writing aspects of advertising, or in business, emphasizing advertising business and management. Included with each listing is the degree(s) obtainable at each institution, its number of advertising graduates, its full-time faculty, scholarships available, financial assistance available, entrance requirements, costs, and the name of the person to write to for more information.

JOBS AND SALARIES

Advertising can provide a dynamic and exciting environment in which to work. The employment outlook is perhaps not quite as exciting. Although employment in advertising is expected to increase faster than the average for all occupations through the mid-1990s, most openings will result from replacement of workers who transfer to other occupations or leave the labor force. The highly qualified and experienced applicant will be favored.

Selected Advertising and Related Publications

Advertising Age
740 Rush Street
Chicago, Illinois 60611

Broadcasting
1735 De Sales Street, NW
Washington, D.C. 20036

Editor and Publisher
11 West 19th Street
New York, New York 10011

Industrial Marketing
220 East 42d Street
New York, New York 10017

Magazine Age
255 Park Avenue
New York, New York 10169

Marketing Communications
475 Park Avenue South
New York, New York 10016

Print Magazine
355 Lexington Avenue
New York, New York 10017

Television/Radio Age
1270 Avenue of the
Americas
New York, New York 10020

CHAPTER 16

BOOK AND MAGAZINE PUBLISHING

"American book sales ... will probably double in
volume by the end of the century ..."

Richard Kostelanetz

OF BOOKS, PAST AND PRESENT

If asked to do so, could you define a book? According to
The Encyclopaedia Britannica, a book is a "written (or printed) message of considerable length, meant for public
circulation and recorded on materials ... light yet durable
enough to afford comparatively easy portability." To carry a
message between people is a book's purpose.

The clay tablets of the Sumerians, Babylonians, Assyrians,
and Hittites, then, were books which had to be inscribed
when wet, then dried in the sun or glazed in a kiln. Luckily
for us, they were not easily destroyed. Hundreds of thousands of them have been recovered.

The papyrus rolls of ancient Egypt were books, too. They
had more portability but less durability than clay tablets.
Scribes recorded their messages on papyrus with reed pens
or brushes and colored inks.

During the Hellenistic era certain libraries were reputed
to have had up to 700,000 rolls, and upper class Romans had

121

private libraries, while slave labor, applied to copying, made books available to the less prosperous. In A.D. 300 there were twenty-eight public libraries in Rome, according to a survey made by Constantine.

For centuries manuscripts were prepared by hand. The Chinese and the Japanese used block printing. The invention of the printing press, a major achievement in communication, had a profound effect on human civilization.

Today we take them for granted, but—notwithstanding the electronic media of the twentieth century—what would we do without books? In the room where I am writing these words I see the *Confessions* of St. Augustine, the *Tao te Ching,* Gardner's *Art Through the Ages,* Kakfa's *The Castle,* Conrad's *Heart of Darkness,* Thackeray's *Vanity Fair,* Castenada's *A Separate Reality,* and Chaucer's *Canterbury Tales.* What electronic medium could possibly recreate the actual experience, the emotional, intellectual, and aesthetic experience of reading such books from cover to cover? Print as medium has been designated (and denigrated) as linear, but only the mechanics of printing and reading are linear. The inner experience of the reading flows outward concentrically.

A CONFERENCE ON THE PUBLICATION OF POETRY AND FICTION

"What we are really discussing is the survival of the life of the imagination," said Stanley Kunitz, consultant in poetry for the Library of Congress, at a conference in 1975 with the theme "The Publication of Poetry and Fiction." His remarks reflected the deep concern felt at this conference for the future survival of fiction and poetry.

In 1974, 40,846 titles were published; of these, 30,745 were new books, 2,382 were fiction titles, and 1,155 were new works of poetry or drama. Fiction and poetry, then, comprised less than ten percent of all books published in the United States in 1974. The statistic, poet Peter Davison pointed out with obvious irony, indicated "how deep" the commitment of publishers was to "what is generally known as the cultural life." The great increase of the number of books published, he added, "has visibly coarsened the fiber as well as swollen the output." The growth pressure, he concluded, was stronger than the health and survival pressure, as far as management was concerned. As for conglomeration, publishing firms like Knopf, Random House, Harcourt Brace Jovanovich, Little Brown, Houghton Mifflin, Putnam, Dutton, Simon & Schuster, William Morrow, and others had preferred to give up their independence rather than "their estates."

Publishers' representatives at this conference focused on economic problems. Publishing serious fiction and poetry, they stated, involved a calculated risk. The representative from Doubleday explained that collections of poetry represented a loss of sometimes $10,000 to $15,000 per hardbound collection. Delayed and negative reviews were another problem. Publishers had been forced to cut back on their lists because either the audiences were not there or they were not being reached.

It was further pointed out that the taste of future audiences was being vulgarized by high school reading lists which were predominantly composed of schlock.

Upon one thing everyone at the conference seemed in agreement: that the publishing business was in a state of crisis. Another, that our education system was not creating a literate public. A third, that the survival of serious writers and poets was problematical.

Their solution? Support for the writer from organizations and foundations in the form of fellowships and grants, and gainful employment at writing-related jobs (teaching, writers-in residence and residencies in small communities to stimulate literary interests and production there).

Since 1975, when this conference was held, the problems aired there have persisted and worsened, and federal money in support of the arts has been cut back.

In 1987, although the book publishing industry was generally in a state of upheaval and was grappling with the belt-tightening effects of continuing conglomeritis, *Publishers Weekly* statistics for 1986 revealed that 52,637 books (consisting of new titles and new editions) were published in the United States—the next to the highest number ever. Of these, the largest category was "Sociology and Economics," with 7,912 books, followed by "Fiction," with 5,578 books. Poetry and drama combined totaled 1,278 books.

An event surely heartening to new fiction writers was the spring and summer "new harvest of first fiction" which was to include 182 new novels, according to the March 15, 1987, *Library Journal.* Of the forty-seven publishers involved, St. Martin's Press led with twenty-five novels, followed by Viking (eleven), Walker (ten), Morrow (eight), Pocket Books (seven), Avon (seven), and Scribner's (seven).

WRITING AND EDITING OPPORTUNITIES IN BOOK PUBLISHING

In the upper echelons of editorial departments of book publishing houses, the work requires very little writing.

Editors

Acquisition editors are concerned with the mechanics (and art) of book selection. Thereafter they negotiate with authors and/or agents, procuring manuscripts on schedule and seeing them through the production process. *Assistant and associate editors* have similar responsibilities, but on a lesser scale and with less autonomy. The *editorial assistant's* job often serves as an apprenticeship. He or she answers the phone, types letters and contracts, files, and acts as a sort of glorified secretary. In the case of books initiated by the publisher, a *developmental editor* may be involved in selection and writing. The *copy editor* is concerned with grammatical correctness, logical and stylistic consistency, phrasing, and word use; he or she may also do proofreading and other duties connected with preparation for printing.

In advertising, sales, and publicity, only the *copywriter* writes; the work includes writing advertising copy, press releases, and the synopses found on book jackets, called flap copy.

How Much Can You Earn?

Publishing houses are not noted for generous salaries. Salary offers quoted in *Publishers Weekly* show that acquisitions editors might be paid from $25,000 to $60,000 or more, copy editors receive $15,000 (at entry level) and a high of around $22,000, and assistant editors earn from $16,000 to $20,000. A copywriter in the marketing and publicity department might earn from $16,000 to $35,000.

OPPORTUNITIES IN MAGAZINE PUBLISHING

Magazine publishers employ editorial assistants, researchers, reporters, copyreaders, writers, and junior and senior editors. A background in newspaper writing is not necessarily desirable or relevant in magazine publishing. There is a qualitative difference: newspaper writing must be objective, factual, and speedily composed to meet deadlines, whereas magazine writing can be subjective, imaginative, colorful, emotional, amusing, cautionary, and individualistic. Usually a magazine story is the collective achievement of several people involved in writing and polishing it.

High school and college students who have worked as yearbook staff members doing layout, writing, copyfitting, photography, editing, and typography have a running start toward a career in the magazine industry.

Because magazines cover the whole spectrum of contemporary areas and issues, a strong, broad liberal arts education is important for magazine journalists. Courses in economics, literature, science, philosophy, sociology, and political science will provide valuable background.

GETTING EDUCATED FOR THE BOOK AND MAGAZINE MARKET

For information about institutions and associations offering courses relative to employment in book and magazine publishing, write the Newspaper Fund for a copy of their *Journalism Career and Scholarship Guide;* or consult *Literary Market Place* under "Courses, Conferences, and Contests." Your library probably has a copy.

Suggested References

Appelbaum, Judith, and Nancy Evans. *How to Get Happily Published.* New York: Harper, 1978.

West, Celeste, and Valerie Wheat. *The Passionate Perils of Publishing.* San Francisco: Booklegger Press, 1978.

Balkin, Richard. *A Writer's Guide to Book Publishing.* New York: Hawthorn Books.

Boswell, John. *The Awful Truth about Publishing.* 1986.

Fulton, Len, ed. *International Dictionary of Little Magazines and Small Presses.* Paradiso: 1987–88.
The Writer's Market
Publishers Weekly
Literary Market Place (LMP)
Carter, Robert A. *Opportunities in Book Publishing Careers.*
Pattis, S. William. *Opportunities in Magazine Publishing Careers.*

Business communicators often are called upon to give presentations.
(IBM photo)

CHAPTER 17

BUSINESS COMMUNICATION AND SCIENCE WRITING

BUSINESS COMMUNICATION

"Those grinning mug shots and cutesy baby photos, bowling team scores and pompous pep talks on productivity have all but disappeared," at least from progressive organizations' publications, according to the International Association of Business Communicators (IABC). Sharp writing, fine photojournalism, creative design, and outstanding art work have replaced them.

The IABC also states, "Today's business communicator is better educated, better paid and more actively involved in management and decision-making." Eight out of ten business communicators have direct access to the top person in the organization, and one in three feels he or she has significant influence in policy-making.

Profile 87, a comprehensive study of the organizational communications profession, presented the following picture of the typical communicator, a majority of whom are women: Most are about thirty years old, have been in the profession about eight years, but at their current job two years; they are college graduates who may have a master's degree or a Ph.D. to their credit; they are part of middle management and work in a major metropolitan area. In addition, they consider their salary commensurate with their duties and responsibilities and as good as, if not better than, salaries of others in similar positions in other organizations. Their title may be *director, manager,* or even *editor.* They came into organizational communication from a newspaper (or straight out of school). In three to five years, they believe, they will be working for another organization.

What type of organization will they choose? Here are the current statistics:

Corporation	40.1%
Association/not for profit	11.9%
Financial institution	9.8%
Hospital/medical	7.4%
PR/communication consultants	6.5%
Educational institution	6.4%
Self	4.6%
Government	4.0%
Labor union	.2%
State owned	.2%
Other	8.9%

What does the typical business communicator earn? In 1987, the median salary was about $32,200 (while men were averaging $42,700). There have been events having a negative impact on communicators generally, such as corporate takeovers, divestiture, buy outs, layoffs, and downsizing, and there has been a decline in the number of communicators on staff in the corporate world from 43.4 percent in 1985, to just over 40 percent in 1987.

Business communicators work under many different department titles—titles which serve to describe their function and type of work:

Communication	30.2%

Public Relations 19.1%
Marketing/Advertising 8.2%
Public Affairs 7.7%
Internal Communication 5.3%
Personnel/Human Resources 4.8%
Corporate Relations 3.2%
Public Information 2.4%
Community Relations 1.6%
Administration 8%
Video 3%
Other 16.4%

What does a business communicator do? Below are some of the daily activities that might occupy her or him, with those activities involving writing listed first:

- Write a speech, give a presentation.
- Edit a publication (from a slick four-color magazine to a low budget, one-page newsletter).
- Interview (everyone from the president to the janitor).
- Produce a multi-media show, design a brochure, conduct a survey.
- Set up an employee-management rap session.

The communications director might also write a screen-script, direct the picture-taking, prepare audio segments, and oversee the final editing. Or he or she might be called upon to prepare safety posters for workers or a script for a closed-circuit TV announcement.

If you want to become a business communicator, IABC suggests the following:

- Continue with your journalism studies.
- Consider courses in economics, finance, management, sociology, and public speaking.
- Get as much practical experience as possible while still in school. (Work on the school newspaper, yearbook, or

the alumni magazine; work in the campus public information office.)
• Investigate internship opportunities in your area.

Your Education/Continuing Education

Many IABC members spend from three to five hours a week on professional development activities. It might be important to your education plans to consider which skills they consider very important.

Advanced communication skills 70.0%
Communication management 59.0%
Basic communication skills 60.3%
Audio-visual/video training 40.6%
General management 35.9%
Case study problem solving 37.3%
Technological developments 32.8%
Research 26.1%

Business communication courses fit into the journalism curricula of various schools in a variety of ways.

At Harvard University, for example, the Communication Arts and Sciences Department had the following courses listed in their bulletin: Communication Theory, Organizational Communication, Mass Communication Practicum, Film Production Arts, Media Research Methods, TV Directing and Lab, Script Writing, Cinematography, Documentary Film, Creative Writing for Film, and other courses.

At the University of Minnesota the Department of Journalism and Mass Communication (graduate school) offered such courses as Magazine Editing and Production, Publications Graphics, Graphic Design Analysis, Photographic Communication, Advanced Photojournalism, Public Relations, Seminar in Mass Communication Research, and other relevant courses.

Suggested Reading

Case Studies in Organization Communication. Industrial Communications Council and Towers, Perrin, Forster, and Crosby, 1975.

Ferguson, Rowena. *Editing the Small Magazine.* Columbia University Press, 1976.

Darrow, Ralph. *House Journal Editing.* Danville: Interstate Printers, 1974.

Lesly, Philip. *Public Relations Handbook.* New York: Prentice Hall, 1978.

Drucker, Peter F. *The Concept of the Corporation.* Mentor, 1963.

Deen, Robert L. *Opportunities in Business Communication Careers.* Lincolnwood, Ill.: VGM Career Horizons, 1987.

SCIENCE WRITING

Science shapes and reshapes our culture and touches and alters our lives. Science writing is a significant part of journalism. An informed public is better able to protect and promote its interests if it understands the issues it may be called upon to advocate or oppose. Why do people read science articles and listen to radio and television broadcast news and special programs? Perhaps because they are aware of the potential impact new discoveries may have on their lives; perhaps because they want to be enlightened about every aspect of the universe in which they live; perhaps because science is intriguing and exciting, and although they may not want to study its intricacies and technicalities, they want to know in general what the scientific world is up to and where it is taking us.

Must Science Writers Be Scientists?

Carl Sagan is an astrophysicist. If you have read *The Dragons of Eden, Broca's Brain, The Comic Connection,* or *Cosmos* (which became a television series), you know how skillfully Sagan can act as "a bridge between the thoughts, ideas, and ordering processes of science and those of non-scientific culture," as Peter Farago put it in *Science and the Media.*

Isaac Asimov taught microbiology at Boston University. He has written over two hundred books, many of them science fiction, many on subjects of scientific interest such as the neutrinos, the planets, the human brain, the quasar, and extraterrestrial life. He too writes in language clearly accessible to the lay reader.

There are, of course, many other reputable scientists—Jacob Bronowski, Konrad Lorenz, and Thomas Lewis, for example—who have written excellent scientific material for popular consumption. But you don't have to be a Ph.D. to write articles about science. Not that anyone can do it. It would be better if your interest in science and scientific subjects was of long standing and was well bolstered by some solid higher education.

If you feel unsure about your qualifications for science writing, arrange for a scientific adviser to review your material and to advise you on the assignment if necessary.

The science writer is not a technical writer. Science writers write for lay audiences, while technical writers write for specialized professional people.

What Does a Science Writer Do?

Science writers explain science and scientific matters in language comprehensible and interesting to nonspecialists, to people who want to know and understand what is happening in the scientific world. They bring the reader up to date on new research and describe research procedures which have given rise to new scientific developments or achievements. They indicate clearly the theoretical and practical significance of new discoveries such as medical techniques and treatments, drugs, and chemicals.

New probes into outer space; threats to the health and survival of the ecosystem; the struggle for a breakthrough in the problem of AIDS; toxic substances in the air we breathe, the water we drink, and the foods we ingest which threaten the health of the human body; the huge and unresolved problem of radioactive wastes—these are some of the subjects currently confronting the science writer and the public.

The information provided comes from many sources: meetings and conventions of scientific associations, radio and television programs, and articles in the daily papers, magazines, brochures, books, and encyclopedias. It is up to the science writer to gather information as it becomes available. He or she must therefore read—deeply, broadly, and constantly—the flow of new material in scientific journals, institutional reports, books, and news releases. The science writer will want to attend press conferences, interview researchers, and attend meetings and annual conventions conducted by medical and others scientific organizations.

Gathering the information is the first step. Once the writer has fully understood and assimilated its meaning and estimated its social and political significance, he or she must translate it into clear, concise, and informal prose, being careful to present both sides where a controversy occurs and always striving to remain objective.

For Whom Do Science Writers Work?

Metropolitan newspapers employ science writers. On newspapers with large staffs science writers may specialize in a variety of areas such as medicine, environment, the physical sciences, the social sciences, and technology. They also work for print and broadcast media, for government agencies (the Nuclear Regulatory Commission, the Environmental Protection Agency, the National Institutes of Health, and the Department of Energy), for professional societies (the American Chemical Society, the American Institute of Physics) and for such organizations as the Cancer Society and the American Heart Association, for universities and hospitals, for large corporations like General Electric, IBM, and many others.

Free-lance Science Writers

The National Association of Science Writers reports that about twenty percent of its members are free-lance writers. They may suggest stories they would like to write, or they may be assigned stories by publications or media outlets. Outside the newspaper and public information fields, most science writing is done by free-lance writers through magazines, books, and TV and motion picture scripts.

The Science Writer's Educational Background

A strong background in both liberal arts and science is recommended. Basic courses in all the sciences (physical, biological, and social) are essential. Some journalism helps, especially for someone whose goal is to write for the media.

In a book review by Robert Anderson appearing in the *Colombia Journalism Review,* writer Dorothy Nelkin offers her advice to science writers: "Science writers are brokers, framing social reality for their readers and shaping the public consciousness about science-related events." As shapers of the public consciousness, Nelkin warns, writers should beware of corporate rhetoric which indulges in public relations binges, "strategies of control" exercised by scientists and institutions "to ensure favorable copy and to influence the images of science in the press—for their own advantage and profit."

Below are two organizations for professional science writers, as described in the *Encyclopedia of Associations.*

COUNCIL FOR THE ADVANCEMENT OF SCIENCE WRITING

Nonmembership. Operated by a council of 26 science writers, editors, television executives, scientists, and physicians. "Works to increase public understanding of science by upgrading the quality and quantity of science writing and improving the relationship between scientists and the press." Has established training programs in science and medical reporting for journalists. Awards Nate Hazeltine Fellowships in Science Writing. Publishes a Guide to Careers in Science Writing.
618 N. Elmwood
Oak Park, IL 60302

NATIONAL ASSOCIATION OF SCIENCE WRITERS

Writers and editors engaged in the preparation and interpretation of science news for the public. Presents awards; sponsors competitions. **Committees:** Free Lance (services to members); Science Liaison; TV-Press Relations; Vocational. **Publications:** (1) Newsletter, quarterly; (2) Awards, annual; also publishes Guide to Careers in Science Writing and Handbook for Press Arrangements at Scientific Meetings. **Affiliated With:** Council for Advancement of Science Writing.

CHAPTER 18

A POSTSCRIPT

Before you make the big decision to try a writing career, it might be well to take an objective look at yourself and ask yourself these hard but important final questions.

1. Are you seriously interested in writing and not primarily motivated by the glamour of success (talk shows, possible screen versions of your book), or by the idea of striking it rich with a blockbuster?

2. How long have you been interested in writing? Long enough to have read widely and deeply into the great literature of the world? Long enough to have tested your interest by writing for the high school literary magazine? The college daily newspaper? Is it a seasoned or a sudden interest?

3. Do you believe you have the talent to make an original contribution in the field of writing?

4. As a free-lance writer, would you have the self-discipline and stamina to work for long periods of time in total isolation?

5. As a salaried writer, do you think you could sustain your creativity in a professional, dependable manner?

6. Could you tolerate the insecurity of working as a free-lancer with no specified income, no regular salary check, and no fringe benefits?
7. Do you consider yourself sufficiently aggressive and determined to take care of the marketing as well as the artistry of your profession?
8. Will your enthusiasm and self-confidence sustain you in the face of criticism and rejection?
9. Could you maintain the quality of your work under the pressure of deadlines sometimes imposed by editors, publishers, or other employers?

Did you answer "yes" to all nine questions? In that case, welcome to the writer's world, where you will find new paths to be explored, rewards to be reaped, and a culture to be informed and enriched. And I would hope that as you write, you will remember these words of Stephen Vincent Benet:

> A writer's theme must, above all, be something he believes in and will defend; something he knows, and knows is worth the labor of writing about.

APPENDIX A

BIBLIOGRAPHY

Abbe, George, ed. *Stephen Vincent Benet on Writing.* Brattleboro: The Stephen Greene Press, 1964.

Asimov, Janet. *How to Enjoy Writing: A Book of Aid and Comfort,* 1987.

Atchity, Kenneth J. *The Writers Time,* 1986.

Barzun, Jacques. *Simple and Direct: A Rhetoric for Writers,* 1981.

Brady, John. *The Craft of Interviewing.* Cincinnati: Writer's Digest, 1976.

Dembo, L. S. and Cyrena N. Pondrom, eds. *The Contemporary Writer: Interviews with Sixteen Novelists.* Madison: The University of Wisconsin Press, 1972.

Flaubert, Gustav. "Letters to Louise Colet." In *The Selected Letters of Gustave Flaubert,* edited by Francis Steegmuller. Reprinted by permission of Farrar, Straus, and Giroux, Inc.

Forester, C. S. *Long Before Forty.* Boston: Little, Brown and Company, 1967.

Golden, Stephen. *The Business of Being a Writer,* 1982.

Hersey, John. *The Writer's Craft.*

James, Henry. *The Notebooks of Henry James.* Edited by F. O. Matthiessen and Kenneth B. Murdock. New York: Oxford University Press, 1947.

Kostelanetz, Richard. *The End of Intelligent Writing.* New York: Sheed and Ward, Inc., 1974.

Longinus, Cassius. *On Great Writing.* New York: The Liberal Arts Press, 1957.

Mann, Thomas. *The Story of a Novel.*

Mott, Frank Luther. *A History of American Magazines.* Cambridge: Harvard University Press, 1957.

Olson, Tillie. *Silences.*

Powers, Ron. *The Newscasters.* New York: St. Martin's Press, 1977.

Quinn, Arthur Hobson. *The Literature of the American People.* New York: Appleton-Century-Crofts, Inc., 1951.

Rivers, William L. *The Mass Media.* New York: Harper and Row, 1975.

Ruas, Charles. *Conversations with American Writers,* 1985.

Sinclair, Upton. *Money Writes.* New York: Albert and Charles Boni, 1927.

Stevenson, Robert Louis. *Learning to Write.* New York: Charles Scribner's Sons, 1920.

Tebbel, John. *The American Magazine: A Compact History.* New York: Hawthorn Books, 1969.

Twain, Mark. *On the Art of Writing.* Edited by M. B. Fried. Buffalo: The Salisbury Club, 1961.

Vivante, Arturo. *Writing Fiction.* Boston: The Writer, Inc., 1980.

Woolf, Virginia. *A Writer's Diary. The Paris Review.*

_____. *Writers at Work.* Edited by George Plimpton. New York: The Viking Press, 1976.

Woolley, Edward Mott. *Freelancing for Forty Magazines.* Norwood: The Plimpton Press, 1927.

APPENDIX B

WRITERS' ORGANIZATIONS AND ASSOCIATIONS

Academy of American Poets
   177 East 87th Street
   New York, New York 10128

American Science Fiction Association
   421 East Carson, #95
   Las Vegas, Nevada 89101

American Society of Journalists and Authors
   1501 Broadway, Suite 1907
   New York, New York 10036

Associated Business Writers of America
   1450 South Havana, Suite 620
   Aurora, Colorado 80012

Dramatists Guild
   234 West 54th Street
   New York, New York 10036

Feminist Writers' Guild
   P.O. Box 14055
   Chicago, Illinois 60614

Mystery Writers of America
   236 West 27th Street
   New York, New York 10001

National Association of Science Writers
   P.O. Box 294
   Greenlawn, New York 11740

National Writers Club
   1450 South Havana, Suite 620
   Aurora, Colorado 80012

The Newspaper Guild
   1125 15th Street, NW
   Washington, D.C. 20005

Poetry Society of America
   15 Grammercy Park
   New York, New York 10003

Poets and Writers
   201 West 54th Street
   New York, New York 10019

Science Fiction Writers of America
   P.O. Box H
   Wharton, New Jersey 07885

Society of Children's Book Writers
   P.O. Box 296, Mar Vista Station
   Los Angeles, California 90066

Society for Technical Communication
   815 15th Street, NW, Suite 506
   Washington, D.C. 20005

Western Writers of America
   1753 Victoria
   Sheridan, Wyoming 82801

Women Writers West
   Box 1637
   Santa Monica, California 90400

Writers Guild of America, East
   555 West 57th Street
   New York, New York 10019

Writers Guild of America, West
  8955 Beverly Boulevard
  Los Angeles, California 90048

Associations with Career Information

American Advertising Association
  1400 K Street, NW, Suite 1000
  Washington, D.C. 20005

American Association of Advertising Agencies
  666 Third Avenue, 13th Fl.
  New York, New York, 10017

American Booksellers Association
  122 East 42d Street
  New York, New York 10168

Accrediting Council on Education in Journalism and Mass
    Communications
  School of Journalism
  University of Kansas
  Lawrence, Kansas 66045

American Newspaper Publishers Association
  The Newspaper Center
  Box 17407
  Dulles International Airport
  Washington, D.C. 20041

Association of American Publishers
  2005 Massachusetts Avenue, NW
  Washington, D.C. 20036

Association for Education in Journalism and Mass Communication
  College of Journalism
  1621 College Street
  University of South Carolina
  Columbia, South Carolina 29208

Business/Professional Advertising Association
  205 East 42d Street
  New York, New York 10017

Council for the Advancement of Science Writers
    618 North Elmood
    Oak Park, Illinois 60302

Dow Jones Newspaper Fund
    P.O. Box 300
    Princeton, New Jersey 08543

Magazine Publishers Association
    575 Lexington Avenue
    New York, New York 10022

National Association of Science Writers
    236 West 27th Street
    New York, New York 10001

Public Relations Society of America
    845 Third Avenue
    New York, New York 10022

Society of Professional Journalists, Sigma Delta Chi
    53 West Jackson Boulevard, Suite 731
    Chicago, Illinois 60604

Society for Technical Communication
    815 15th Street, NW, Suite 506
    Washington, D.C. 20005

Women in Communications, Inc.
    P.O. Box 9561
    Austin, Texas 78766

VGM CAREER BOOKS

OPPORTUNITIES IN

*Available in both
paperback and hardbound
editions*
Accounting Careers
Acting Careers
Advertising Careers
Agriculture Careers
Airline Careers
Animal and Pet Care
Appraising Valuation Science
Architecture
Automotive Service
Banking
Beauty Culture
Biological Sciences
Book Publishing Careers
Broadcasting Careers
Building Construction Trades
Business Communication Careers
Business Management
Cable Television
Carpentry Careers
Chemical Engineering
Chemistry Careers
Child Care Careers
Chiropractic Health Care
Civil Engineering Careers
Commercial Art and Graphic
  Design
Computer Aided Design
  and Computer Aided Mfg.
Computer Maintenance Careers
Computer Science Careers
Counseling & Development
Crafts Careers
Dance
Data Processing Careers
Dental Care
Drafting Careers
Electrical Trades
Electronic and Electrical
  Engineering
Energy Careers
Engineering Technology Careers
Environmental Careers
Fashion Careers
Federal Government Careers
Film Careers
Financial Careers
Fire Protection Services
Fitness Careers
Food Services
Foreign Language Careers
Forestry Careers
Gerontology Careers
Government Service
Graphic Communications

Health and
  Medical Careers
High Tech Careers
Home Economics Careers
Hospital Administration
Hotel & Motel Management
Industrial Design
Insurance Careers
Interior Design
International Business
Journalism Careers
Landscape Architecture
Laser Technology
Law Careers
Law Enforcement and
  Criminal Justice
Library and Information
  Science
Machine Trades
Magazine Publishing Careers
Management
Marine & Maritime Careers
Marketing Careers
Materials Science
Mechanical Engineering
Microelectronics
Modeling Careers
Music Careers
Nursing Careers
Nutrition Careers
Occupational Therapy
  Careers
Office Occupations
Opticianry
Optometry
Packaging Science
Paralegal Careers
Paramedical Careers
Part-time & Summer Jobs
Personnel Management
Pharmacy Careers
Photography
Physical Therapy Careers
Plumbing & Pipe Fitting
Podiatric Medicine
Printing Careers
Psychiatry
Psychology
Public Health Careers
Public Relations Careers
Real Estate
Recreation and Leisure
Refrigeration and
  Air Conditioning
Religious Service
Retailing
Robotics Careers
Sales Careers

Sales & Marketing
Secretarial Careers
Securities Industry
Social Work Careers
Speech-Language Pathology
  Careers
Sports & Athletics
Sports Medicine
State and Local Government
Teaching Careers
Technical Communications
Telecommunications
Television and Video Careers
Theatrical Design
  & Production
Transportation Careers
Travel Careers
Veterinary Medicine Careers
Vocational and Technical Careers
Word Processing
Writing Careers
Your Own Service Business

CAREERS IN

Accounting
Business
Communications
Computers
Health Care
Science

CAREER DIRECTORIES

Careers Encyclopedia
Occupational Outlook Handbook

CAREER PLANNING

How to Get and Get Ahead
  On Your First Job
How to Get People to Do
  Things Your Way
How to Have a Winning
  Job Interview
How to Land a Better Job
How to Write a Winning Résumé
Joyce Lain Kennedy's Career Book
Life Plan
Planning Your Career Change
Planning Your Career of
  Tomorrow
Planning Your College Education
Planning Your Military Career
Planning Your Own Home
  Business
Planning Your Young Child's
  Education

SURVIVAL GUIDES

High School Survival Guide
College Survival Guide

VGM Career Horizons
a division of *NTC Publishing Group*
4255 West Touhy Avenue